Antigua, Montserrat & St Kitts

Sarah Cameron

Credits

Footprint credits
Editor: Nicola Gibbs
Production and layout: Emma Bryers
Maps: Kevin Feeney

Publisher: Patrick Dawson
Managing Editor: Felicity Laughton
Advertising: Elizabeth Taylor
Sales and marketing: Kirsty Holmes

Photography credits
Front cover: Jason Patrick Ross/
Shutterstock.com
Back cover: Superstock/Gavin Hellier/
Robert Harding Picture Library

Printed in India by Thomson Press Ltd,
Faridabad, Haryana

Every effort has been made to ensure
that the facts in this guidebook are
accurate. However, travellers should
still obtain advice from consulates,
airlines, etc, about travel and visa
requirements before travelling. The
authors and publishers cannot accept
responsibility for any loss, injury or
inconvenience however caused.

The content of Footprint *Focus
Antigua, Montserrat & St Kitts* has been
based on Footprint's *Caribbean Island
Handbook*, which was researched and
written by Sarah Cameron.

Publishing information
Footprint *Focus Antigua, Montserrat &
St Kitts*
1st edition
© Footprint Handbooks Ltd
September 2014

ISBN: 978 1 909268 34 0
CIP DATA: A catalogue record
for this book is available from
the British Library

® Footprint Handbooks and the
Footprint mark are a registered
trademark of Footprint Handbooks Ltd

Published by Footprint
6 Riverside Court
Lower Bristol Road
Bath BA2 3DZ, UK
T +44 (0)1225 469141
F +44 (0)1225 469461
footprinttravelguides.com

Distributed in the USA by
National Book Network, Inc.

Contents

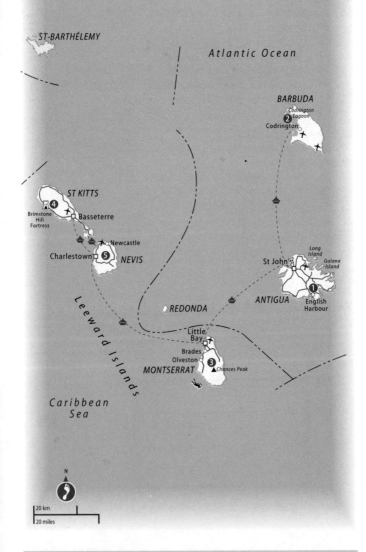

ST-BARTHÉLEMY

Atlantic Ocean

BARBUDA
Codrington
Lagoon
② Codrington ✈

ST KITTS
♜④
Brimstone
Hill
Fortress
□ Basseterre
✈ Newcastle
Charlestown □ ⑤ NEVIS

Long
Island
St John's ✚ Guiana
Island
① ANTIGUA
English
Harbour

L
e
e
w
a
r
d

I
s
l
a
n
d
s

♦ REDONDA

Little
Bay
Brades
Olveston ③ ▲ Chances Peak
MONTSERRAT

Caribbean
Sea

N
▲
🦶

20 km
20 miles

4 ● Antigua, Montserrat & St Kitts

Antigua, Barbuda, Montserrat, St Kitts and Nevis are part of the Leeward Islands, a geographical grouping of small, mostly volcanic islands in the northeastern Caribbean. They share a chequered history of territorial struggles between European powers before becoming British colonies, with sugar plantations and slavery. Their geo-political importance in the 18th and 19th centuries can still be seen in their beautifully preserved fortifications, particularly at English Harbour and Nelson's Dockyard in Antigua and Brimstone Hill Fortress on St Kitts. Sailing vessels still fill the harbours of Antigua, but for more peaceful purposes. Regattas attract hundreds of yachts and their crews, who come ashore to party just like the sailors of old. Most visitors, however, arrive by air in search of sun, sea and sand. Antigua and St Kitts both receive long-haul flights, with smaller planes fanning out from these hubs to connect with the other islands. This makes it easy to island hop and plan a two- or three-centre holiday. From Antigua it is easy to visit Barbuda and Montserrat, while St Kitts is paired with Nevis.

Dependence on sugar is long gone and tourism is now king. The coastline of Antigua curves into coves and graceful harbours with 365 soft white-sand beaches, among the most attractive in the West Indies. Its sister island, Barbuda, is blessed with a swathe of white sand stretching for 17 miles down its empty west coast – except where it is pink from crushed shells. St Kitts has powder-soft sandy beaches all round its hilly southeastern peninsula, while the west coast of Nevis is similarly endowed. Montserrat is different, however, boasting black sand on all but one of its beaches and for good reason: it is volcanic and the volcano is active. Yet, while beaches are not its main selling point, Montserrat does attract visitors to its waters, which are teeming with fish, coral and sponges; while onland, hikers and birdwatchers are rewarded by the island's bountiful flora and fauna in the hilly tropical forests.

Planning your trip

Best time to visit the Leeward Islands

The climate everywhere in the Caribbean is tropical, with variations in rainfall. The volcanic, mountainous and forested islands attract more rain than the low-lying coral islands, so you can expect frequent showers in Montserrat but not on Barbuda. The driest and coolest time of year is usually December-April, which is also the peak tourist season. However there can be showers, which keep things green. Temperatures during this time can fall to 20°C during the day, depending on altitude, but are normally in the high 20s. The mean annual temperature is about 26°C. At other times of the year the temperature rises only slightly, but greater humidity can make it feel hotter if you are away from the coast, where the northeast trade winds are a cooling influence. The main climate hazard is hurricane season (see box, page 8), which runs from June to November, although storms are rare before September. The Leeward Islands are frequent victims of autumn storms, which build up in the southern Atlantic before sweeping across the island arc towards the USA.

Getting to the Leeward Islands

Air
Long-haul flights from North America and the UK arrive in Antigua and St Kitts, from where you can get onward flights to other islands. There are scheduled and charter flights and you can often pick up good-value deals on package holidays. **VC Bird International Airport** (see page 57) is in the northeast corner of Antigua, allowing passengers with window seats an enticing view of the coastline and multi-hued waters around the island as the plane comes in to land. The **Robert L Bradshaw International Airport** (see page 114) on St Kitts is in the middle of the island, close to the capital, Basseterre, and on arrival you get a good view of the Caribbean coastline including several historic fortresses. The airports on Nevis and Montserrat receive regional carriers, while Barbuda's small airport is for domestic services only.

Flights from the UK British Airways (www.ba.com) has a daily service from London to Antigua. It operates a code share with **Caribbean Airlines** (www.caribbean-airlines.com), allowing onward connections to the southern Caribbean. **Virgin Atlantic** (www.virgin-atlantic.com) flies twice a week to Antigua from London and both these airlines offer connecting

Don't miss...

1 English Harbour, Antigua, page 35.
2 Frigate Bird Sanctuary, Barbuda, page 40.
3 Soufrière Hills Volcano, Montserrat, page 69.
4 Brimstone Hill Fortress, St Kitts, page 90.
5 Nevis Peak hike, Nevis, page 113.

Numbers relate to the map on page 4.

services to and from Europe. You can also fly on from Antigua to Nevis with **Fly Montserrat** (www.flymontserrat.com). **British Airways** flies twice a week from London to St Kitts.

Flights from Europe KLM (www.klm.com) flies from Amsterdam to Sint Maarten and **Air France** (www.airfrance.co.uk) flies from Paris to Sint Maarten, from where you can get connecting flights, eg with **Winair** (www.fly-winair.sx) to Nevis.

Flights from North America There are direct flights to the Caribbean from the USA and Canada with connecting flights via San Juan and Sint Maarten to Antigua and/or St Kitts. **American Airlines** (www.aa.com), **Delta** (www.delta.com), **Continental** (www.continental.com), **US Airways** (www.usairways.com) and **Caribbean Airlines** all fly from the USA; **Air Canada** (www.aircanada.com) offers services from Canada.

Flights from the Caribbean The main carrier is LIAT (www.liatairline.com), which connects nearly all the islands of the Caribbean with its hub in Antigua, including St Kitts and Nevis. Other airlines offering regional services include **Caribbean Airlines**, flying between Antigua, Barbados, Trinidad and Tobago, Guyana and Suriname; **Seaborne Airways** (www.seaborneairways.com) flies from San Juan to St Kitts and Nevis; **Cape Air** (www.capeair.com) and **Tradewind Aviation** (www.tradewindaviation.com) fly from San Juan to Nevis; **Air Sunshine** (www.airsunshine.com) flies from San Juan, St Thomas and Tortola to St Kitts and Nevis and from San Juan and St Thomas to Antigua; **Winair** (www.fly-winair.sx) flies from Sint Maarten to St Kitts and Nevis; **Fly Montserrat** (www.flymontserrat.com) and **ABM Air** (part of SVG Air, www.svgair.com, http://montserrat-flights.com) fly from Antigua to Montserrat and Barbuda. These regional airlines also offer charter services for island hopping at your convenience.

Hurricane season

June too soon, July stand by, August you must, September remember, October all over.

From the 1950s to the 1980s there was little hurricane activity in the region and homes were not built to withstand severe storms. In 1989 this all started to change when several violent storms roared through the islands and Hurricane Hugo did untold damage. The next few years were relatively quiet but 1995 struck with a bang and was the start of a 10-year period that has gone down in history as the most active on record. Analysts expect that this active hurricane era will last another two or three decades, with storms increasing in intensity. In recent years there have been several late storms and the 'October all over' saying proved a myth.

In weather forecasts, a **tropical depression** is an organized system of clouds and thunderstorms with a defined circulation and maximum sustained winds of 38 mph (33 knots) or less; a **tropical storm** is an organized system of strong thunderstorms with a defined circulation and maximum sustained winds of 39-73 mph (34-63 knots); a **hurricane** is an intense tropical weather system with a well-defined circulation and maximum sustained winds of 74 mph (64 knots) or more.

A hurricane develops in warm waters and air, which is why the tropics are known for hurricanes. Powered by heat from the sea they are steered by the easterly trade winds and the temperate westerly winds, as well as their own ferocious energy. In the Atlantic, these storms form off the African coast and move west, developing as they come into warmer water. The process by which a 'disturbance' strengthens into a hurricane depends on at least three conditions: warm water, moisture and wind pattern near the ocean surface that spirals air inward. Bands of thunderstorms form and allow the air to warm further and rise higher into the atmosphere. If the winds at these higher levels are light, the structure remains intact and allows further strengthening. If the winds are strong, they will shear off the top and stop the development. If the system develops, a definite eye is formed around which the most violent activity takes place; this is known as the eyewall. The centre of the eye is relatively calm. When the eye passes over land those on the ground often think that the hurricane is over; some even abandon safe shelter, not aware that as the eye passes, the other half of the hurricane is yet to come. At the top of the eyewall (around 50,000 ft), most of the air is propelled outward, increasing the air's upward motion.

The word 'hurricane' is derived from the Amerindian 'Hurakan', both the Carib god of evil and also one of the Maya creator gods who blew his breath across the chaotic water and brought forth dry land. In the North Atlantic, Gulf of Mexico, Caribbean and the Eastern Pacific they are called hurricanes, in Australia, cyclones or 'willy willy', and in the Philippines, 'baguio'. In the Western North Pacific tropical cyclones of hurricane force are called typhoons. The first time hurricanes were named was by an Australian forecaster in the early 1900s who called them after political figures he disliked. During the Second World War, US Army forecasters named storms after their girlfriends and wives. Today names (male and female) are chosen by the National Hurricane Center in Miami (www.nhc.noaa.gov/) and submitted to the World Meteorology Organization in Geneva. As a system develops, it is assigned a name in alphabetical order from the official list.

These days, there is very good information, thanks to accurate weather data gathered by the Hurricane Hunters from Keesler Airforce Base in the USA. Most of the islands are now well prepared to cope with hurricanes and have disaster relief teams in place, while many of the island resorts, especially the larger ones, have their own generators and water supplies.

While a hurricane can certainly pose a threat to life, risks are reduced if precautions are taken. The main hazards include storm surge, heavy winds and rains. There is usually disruption of services such as communications, internal transport and airline services. If a hurricane is approaching, it is best for tourists to evacuate the island. Hurricanes usually last six to 36 hours and you have to be shut up inside a closed area, often with little ventilation or light, which can be stressful. Some tourists think a hurricane will be 'fun' and want to remain on island to see the storm. This is not a good idea. If you do remain you should register with your local consulate or embassy and email home as soon as the warning is given to alert your family that communications may go down. Always follow the rules of the emergency services and be prepared to help out in the clearing up afterwards.

As violent weather approaches, the local Met office issues advisories:

Tropical storm watch Be on alert for a storm (winds of 39-73 mph) which may pose threats to coastal areas within 36 hours.

Tropical storm warning The storm is expected within 24 hours.

Hurricane watch Hurricane conditions could be coming in 36 hours.

Hurricane warning The hurricane is expected within 24 hours.

One of the best internet sites for information during a hurricane is www.stormcarib.com. The website www.hurricanehunters.com has a virtual reality flight into the eye of a hurricane.

Sea

Large cruise ships call at Antigua and St Kitts as part of their eastern Caribbean itineraries, while smaller ships visit Nevis and Montserrat. There is no long-distance ferry service throughout the entire Caribbean, but inter-island ferries are available. **M&M Transportation** operates three vessels: MV *Caribe Sun*, the largest with 194 passengers; MV *Caribe Surf*, the next biggest; and MV *Caribe Breeze*. These ships connect Montserrat with Antigua, St Kitts and Nevis. Applications are being made with the French authorities to allow MV *Caribe Sun* to connect Montserrat with Guadeloupe. In 2014, the ferry sailed between Montserrat and Antigua Wednesday-Sunday, departing Montserrat 0630, 1½ hours, with two crossings on Wednesday/Friday/Sunday and one on Thursday/Saturday. Fares are EC\$150 one way, EC\$300 return (half price for children aged two to 12, EC\$5 for infants under two), plus EC\$45 tax for non-nationals and EC\$10 security charge. These are international services and normal immigration and customs regulations apply. Check-in is 1½ hours before departure from Antigua and one hour when leaving Montserrat. You do not need to buy tickets in advance. For further information, contact the agents in Montserrat: Roosevelt Jemmotte, T664-496 9912; or in Antigua: Jennifer Burke, T268-778 9786. The ferry between St Kitts and Montserrat is less frequent, leaving St Kitts on Wednesday morning and returning from Montserrat on Sunday evening. Contact Captain Prince Mills, T869-662 3258, princemills@hotmail.com.

Transport in the Leeward Islands

Air

There are domestic flights between the sister islands of Antigua and Barbuda. Charter flights are also available which can be useful if you are in a group of five or more. To get to Barbuda, you can either take the more-or-less regular 15-minute **ABM** flight which leaves Antigua early morning or in the afternoon, allowing a day trip (EC\$300 return) or, if you are staying at either of Barbuda's two hotels, they will arrange transport for their guests. It is best to stay on Antigua overnight before flying to Barbuda as international flights mostly arrive after **ABM** has left. Flights can be cancelled at short notice, so be prepared.

Sea

The sister islands of Antigua and Barbuda and St Kitts and Nevis are connected by ferry. The **Barbuda Express** (www.barbudaexpress.com) catamaran runs five days a week except in bad weather. You don't have to book in advance, but it is advisable as then you will be notified of any delays and cancellations. The crossing takes 1½ hours, EC\$260/US\$100 round trip, or US\$169 (US\$85 for children aged three to 12) for a day tour, which includes a boat trip to the lagoon to see the frigate birds, a taxi tour of the island and beach time with a lobster lunch on the sand. Seasickness pills are available on board and are recommended, although the ferry won't run if it is very rough. There is a variety of transport between St Kitts and Nevis by sea. Ferries take 35-45 minutes (EC$20 adult, EC$10 child, plus EC$1 port tax) and leave Basseterre about every two hours Monday-Saturday 0600-1800 (with later crossings Friday/Saturday and fewer crossings on Sunday) docking at Charleston. The **Seabridge Ferry** (passengers and vehicles, EC$75 for car and driver one way, EC$125 round trip, EC$15 additional passengers) leaves from Majors Bay and docks at Cades Bay, 15 minutes, every two hours. Water taxis usually take you from Reggae Beach on St Kitts to Oualie Beach on Nevis, 10 minutes. They cost around US$85-100 during the day, double at night, taking two to five passengers. Some Nevis hotels include this when you book a room and it includes the taxi from the airport to the boat and the taxi at the other end to your hotel (tip the drivers). It is more expensive than taking the ferry but it's much quicker, allows you more flexibility, and your luggage is taken care of.

Road
Roads are generally in good condition on Antigua and St Kitts, although there are often potholes and storm ditches in rural areas and poor signage; local drivers know where they are going and don't need signposts. Traffic can be heavily congested in the capital cities, St John's and Basseterre. Nevis has one 20-mile paved road around the island with smaller access roads off it. Montserrat has a single, hilly main road that winds along the east and west coasts and across the middle. Barbuda only really has one road too, with dirt tracks leading off it to beaches. Driving is on the left although the steering wheel may be on either side. Local drivers often drive fast, ignoring speed restrictions, and use their horns a lot.

Bus Buses, usually minivans, are the principal means of transport for the local people on Antigua and St Kitts and Nevis. The service on Antigua covers only the southern half of the island starting in St John's and there is no service out to the airport. Buses set off when full and run frequently during the day, but rarely after dark or on Sunday. See www.busstopanu.com for routes and fares. On St Kitts buses similarly avoid the areas where tourists might want to go, ie the southeastern peninsula, but routes go out from Basseterre to the north, east and west. On Nevis there is only one road around the island so buses head out from Charleston in both directions. They have green licence plates beginning with H or HA. They can also be recognized by the decorated name painted on the front. A bus may be flagged down anywhere along its route and will drop passengers off anywhere on request. On Montserrat taxis and buses with green H licence plates run along the main road in daylight hours and can be hailed anywhere. There are no fixed schedules or stops. There is no bus service on Barbuda.

Car Car hire is available on all the islands subject to the purchase of a local driving licence on presentation of your licence from home. On Antigua and Barbuda this costs EC$50, valid for three months. On St Kitts and Nevis it is EC$62.50 and on Montserrat EC$50.

Cycling Bike rental is available on all the islands, either through your hotel, car or boat hire companies, watersports operators or a bike rental agency. Some organize mountain bike tours. Cycling is not particularly common, although road racing is popular. You need to be careful of drivers on the roads, always give way to motorized traffic and avoid cycling on Sunday afternoons or public holidays when motorists have had too much to drink. Loose stones and gravel at the edges of roads can be hazardous, as can potholes and storm drains. There are some great donkey or goat trails for off-road riding in places, but acacia thorns can play havoc with your tyres. It is safest to ride in a group, do not cycle after dark, let someone know if you are heading off to a remote area and carry plenty of water.

Taxi Taxis are plentiful and offer tours as well as short journeys. They are not metered, so agree a price in advance. There is usually a list of government-approved fares at the airports. Taxis have TX registration plates on Antigua, yellow T plates on St Kitts and Nevis and green H plates on Montserrat.

Walking The smaller islands of Montserrat, Nevis and Barbuda are the most rewarding for hiking, with lots of paths and trails where you can see the best of the local flora and fauna. Birdwatching is particularly good on Montserrat and hiking tours are offered by naturalists.

Where to stay in the Leeward Islands

There is a wide and varied selection of hotels, guesthouses, apartments and villas. The majority of hotels are small, friendly and offer flexible service. They cater for all budgets, from the height of luxury to simple guesthouses. Youth hostels are non-existent and camping is not allowed.

The cheapest accommodation can be found in **guesthouses**, small, privately run establishments which sometimes offer breakfast but do not rely on a full restaurant service. Many of these are not registered with the local tourist office and therefore difficult to find until you get there. They may be perfectly adequate if you are not very demanding, or they may be flea pits.

Price codes

Where to stay

$$$$ over US$150 $$$ US$66-151
$$ US$30-65 $ under US$30

Price for a double room in high season, rack rate. Hotels will add tax and service to the bill. Sometimes they are included in the quoted rate, so it is worth checking.

Restaurants

$$$ over US$12 $$ US$7-12 $ US$6 and under

Price for a two-course meal for one person, excluding drinks or service charge.

Turning up at a cheaper place may not always yield a room because competition is high. Note also that, if booking ahead, tourist office lists may not include the cheapest establishments, so you may have to reserve one or two nights at a mid-price hotel for when you arrive and then ask around for cheaper accommodation if that is what you want. The longer you stay the better deal you will get, so negotiation is recommended. Remember also that high season runs from mid-December to mid-April and everything is more expensive then as well as being more heavily booked. The best deals can be found in – you guessed it – hurricane season.

On Antigua, the greatest concentration of developments is in the area around St John's, along the coast to the west and also to the north in a clockwise direction to the airport, taking advantage of some of the best beaches. You would only really want to stay in St John's if you were there on business or visiting for a cricket match. A second cluster of hotels is around English Harbour and Falmouth Harbour in the southeast of the island. These are very pleasant with lovely views of the harbours and yachts at anchor. Many may be closed September-October. There are several all-inclusive resorts, most of which are not included in this guide. There are lots of self-catering apartments, but a common complaint is that sufficient provisions are not available locally and you have to go into St John's for shopping, requiring a taxi or car hire. On Barbuda there are only two hotels and accommodation is either expensive and exclusive or basic, with little in between. Several private homes offer lodging. Take mosquito repellent and earplugs if you are staying in the centre of Codrington at weekends. Montserrat also has only a couple of hotels. Most accommodation is in guesthouses or with people who rent out rooms and apartments in their houses. Villa rentals are also available from around US$1000 a week through agencies. St Kitts and Nevis have a wide variety of lodgings from first-class plantation inns and beach hotels to rented cottages. There has been a construction boom in Frigate Bay and the southeast peninsula on St Kitts, which has brought the 640-room **Marriott** hotel and casino, popular with some but quite out of keeping with the rest of the hotels on the island. The largest resort on Nevis is the 218-room **Four Seasons**, complete with spa and golf course, but the other hotels are in the style of old English plantation houses: intimate, stylish and tasteful.

Food and drink in the Leeward Islands

Food As you might expect of islands, there is a wide variety of seafood on offer which is fresh and tasty and served in a multitude of ways. Fish of all sorts, as well as lobster and conch, are commonly available and are usually better quality than local meat. Beef and lamb are often imported from the USA or Argentina, but goat, pork and chicken are produced locally. There is no dairy industry to speak of, so cheeses are also usually imported. There is, however, a riot of tropical fruit and vegetables and a visit to a local market will give you the opportunity to see unusual and often unidentifiable objects as well as more familiar items found in supermarkets in Europe and North America but with 10 times the flavour. They won't all have been grown on these islands but will have come from their neighbours in the Caribbean. The best bananas in the world are grown in the Caribbean on small farms either organically or, at least, using the minimum of chemicals. They are cheap and incredibly sweet and unlike anything you can buy at home. You will come across many of the wonderful tropical fruits in the form of juices or ice cream. Don't miss the rich flavours of the soursop, the guava or the sapodilla. Mangoes in season are found on every breakfast plate. Caribbean oranges are often green when ripe, as there is no cold season to bring out the orange colour, and are meant for juicing not peeling. Portugals are like tangerines and easy to peel. Avocados are nearly always sold unripe, so wait several days before attempting to eat them. Many vegetables have their origins in the slave trade, brought over to provide a starchy diet for the slaves. The breadfruit, a common staple, rich in carbohydrates and vitamins A, B and C, was brought from the South Seas in 1793 by Captain Bligh, perhaps more famous for the mutiny on the *Bounty*.

On Antigua, there are some local specialities, found in smaller restaurants in St John's, which should never be missed: **saltfish** (traditionally eaten at breakfast in a tomato and onion sauce), **pepper-pot** with fungi or *foungee* (a kind of cornmeal dumpling), **goat water** (hot goat stew), **shellfish** (the local name for trunk fish), **conch stew** and the local staple, **chicken and rice**. **Johnny cake** is rather like a savoury doughnut, but you will find variations on the theme in other islands. **Ducana** is made from grated sweet potato and coconut, mixed with pumpkin, sugar and spices and boiled in a banana leaf. **Tropical fruits and vegetables** found on other Caribbean islands are also found here: bread fruit, cristophene, dasheen, eddo, mango, guava and pawpaw (papaya). Oranges are green, while the native pineapple is called the Antigua black and is very sweet. Locally made **Sunshine** ice cream, American-style, is available in most supermarkets.

St Kitts has a wide variety of fresh seafood (red snapper, lobster, kingfish, blue parrot), and local vegetables as well as imported produce. Try some of the local dishes: **conkey** (usually available during Easter), **ital** which the local rastas make (food seasoned with all natural spices, no salt but very delicious), also **black pudding**, **goat water**, **saltfish** and **johnny cakes** and **souse**. They are all foods which Kittitians love to eat, especially on Saturday when no one wants to cook at home. Look out for excellent local patties and fruit juices. Local bakeries have a variety of savoury and sweet baked goods at affordable prices and many have dining sections too.

Drink Imported wines and spirits are reasonably priced but local drinks (fruit and sugar cane juice, coconut milk, and Antiguan rum punches and swizzles, ice cold) must be experienced. The local **Cavalier** rum is a light golden colour, usually used for mixes. Beer can be bought at good prices from most supermarkets and the **Wadadli Brewery** on Crabbs peninsula. There are no licensing restrictions. Tap water is safe only in hotels and resorts; bottled water is available if you are unsure. The excellent local spirit produced in St Kitts by Baron de Rothschild (in a joint venture with **Demerara Distillers Ltd** of Guyana) is **CSR – Cane Spirit Rothschild**. It is drunk neat, with ice or water, or with 'Ting', the local grapefruit soft drink (highly recommended). Tours of the CSR factory are possible.

Eating out Restaurants range from gourmet eateries to cafés but all make the most of local ingredients. If you are economizing, find a local place and choose the daily special, which will give you a chance to try typical local food. Fast food is also available, but you will be better off going to a local place serving chicken and chips or burgers, rather than the international chains. There are not many restaurants on Barbuda and they tend to close in the evening, so check beforehand. Food is cooked at lunchtime and is available until about 1700, or when it runs out. You have to talk to the owner if you want an evening meal. Restaurants tend to close on Sunday in Basseterre, although most of the plantation inns around St Kitts offer Sunday brunch, usually a three-course meal. There are many places offering snacks, light meals, ice cream and drinks in Basseterre and in the Frigate Bay area. On Nevis, the best, upmarket restaurants are in the hotels and it is usually necessary to reserve a table; they offer exceptional cuisine as well as barbecues and entertainment on certain nights of the week. There are very few eating places in Charlestown and none of them is expensive. In low season most restaurants only open in the evenings, and some shut completely. Several places on Montserrat do takeaway meals and there are lots of 'snackettes' where you can pick up a decent local lunch on the side of the road. Bakeries are also good places to get a snack. Some places only open if you make a reservation in advance, so it is best to check. Restaurant opening times are from 0730-1000, 1130-1400 and 1900-2200, although not all are open for breakfast and several only open in the evenings if there is demand.

Entertainment in the Leeward Islands

The largest hotels provide dancing, calypso, steel bands, limbo dancers and moonlight barbecues, so that their guests need never leave the property. Entertainment comes to them, with live music and other acts rotating between the various hotels. On Antigua, the area around English Harbour is the hot spot for tourists, particularly for the yachting fraternity who come ashore for a good time. Most nightlife happens in bars, or restaurants with bars which can host live music. There are a couple of clubs frequented by Antiguans in their 20s, where you can dance into the early hours.

Barbuda is very quiet, although the bars in Codrington can get lively and noisy at weekends. Montserrat's three nightclubs only open at weekends, normally 2100-0200, but there are more than 70 bars, ranging from the simple to the sophisticated, some with pool tables and darts. Bars occasionally present live music featuring calypsonians and other musicians over from Antigua or other islands; these are advertised on the radio, or ask around.

The club scene on St Kitts has no set hours; doors open around 2200 with people arriving at around 2300-2400 and leaving at 0500 when the sun comes up. Most dance floors provide a wide variety of music and entrance costs vary, depending on the occasion, with overseas performers commanding the upper limit. Nightclubs have a great mix of calypso, soca, salsa, hip-hop, reggae, dance hall, R&B, house, techno and other types of music. For the real local experience, visit dance spots out in the country area: **BCA**, T869-465 7606/7, at Saddlers; **Manhattan Gardens**, T869-465 9121, and **Sprat Net**, in Old Road, **Off Limit**, in Cayon, T869-466 9821, and the **Inner Circle Club**, at St Paul's, where action takes place by announcement. These venues are frequented by some of the region's top DJs as well as local bands playing local music.

Nevis is quiet and most visitors content themselves with a good meal in the evening and maybe an after-dinner drink. However, there is entertainment for visitors and locals, particularly at the weekends. Hotels organize activities on different nights in high season. Look for posters, radio announcements or ask what's on at the tourist office.

Antigua

Feb Wadadli Day on the last Sat, this is Antigua's largest cultural festival, held in the Botanical Gardens and showcasing traditional games, such as warri, dancing, calypsonians, steel pan and other live music, local foods such as saltfish, funji, cha cha dumplings and ducana, as well as entertainment for children.

Apr The Classic Yacht Regatta, http://antiguaclassics.com. Spectacular, with yawls, ketches, schooners and square-masted vessels, contact the **Antigua Yacht Club**, T268-460 1799. The **International Kite Festival** is held for a week around Easter, with some amazing creations taking to the skies.

Apr-May Antigua Sailing Week, T268-462 8872, www.sailingweek.com. A huge regatta with participants from over 30 countries, fun events, live music, Nelson's Dockyard.

Jul-Aug Carnival is at the end of Jul and lasts until the 1st Tue in Aug. The main event is '**J'ouvert**', or '**Juvé**' morning when from 0400 people come into town dancing behind steel and brass bands. Carnival takes place in the streets of St John's and at the Antigua Recreation Ground (ARG). There are competitions for the Calypso Monarch with sections for women and children as well as beauty pageants. Hotels and airlines tend to be booked up well in advance. Contact the **Carnival Committee**, High St, St John's, T268-462 4707, http://antiguacarnival.com.

Oct-Nov 2 weeks of preparations build up to **Heritage Day** on 21 Oct. Schools and offices prepare decorations for judging and various events lead up to **National Dress Day** on 31 Oct with a **Food Fair and Exhibition** followed by a ceremonial parade on 1 Nov for **Independence Day**, http://www.independence.gov.ag/.

Barbuda

May Barbuda has a small carnival known as **Caribana**, held over the Whitsun weekend, with beach parties, seafood, horse racing and music and dancing in the streets.

Montserrat

17 Mar St Patrick's Day (a national holiday) is celebrated on the 'Emerald Isle' with concerts, masquerades, story telling, a kite festival, local foods in a 'slave feast' and other festivities lasting for nearly a week. It also commemorates a slave uprising on that day in 1768.

2nd Sat in Jun The **Queen's Birthday** is celebrated with parades, salutes and the raising of flags.

Jul Calabash Festival a week-long festival in the middle of the month named after the gourd from the calabash tree, traditionally used to make musical instruments, bowls and decorative household items. There are hikes, boat tours, cricket, a food fair, lectures, gospel concert and other entertainment.

1st Mon in Aug Emancipation Day commemorating the abolition of slavery in 1834. It is a public holiday and there are beach barbecues and picnics all weekend. **Cudjoe Head Day** on the Sat before emphasizes the island's African heritage, with races, music, masquerades and more. The evening before, there is a street festival with live music and vendors. The village of Cudjoe Head was named after a runaway slave called Cudjoe, who was caught, killed and had his head placed on a silk cotton tree as a warning to others.

Dec The island's main festival is the **Christmas season**, which starts around the first weekend and continues through New Year's Day. There are shows, concerts, calypso competitions, jump-ups and masquerades and of course festivities and parties on **New Year's Eve**, helped down with lots of goat water.

St Kitts
Apr The annual 4-km **Nevis to St Kitts Cross Channel Swim**.
May Green Valley, Cayon, St Kitts, holds a **community festival/carnival** with calypso, parades, competitions and parties.
Jun St Kitts holds a **music festival** at the end of Jun; 4 nights of calypso, reggae, R&B, jazz, street-style, gospel, country and western and rap, with local and famous overseas artists.
Dec The liveliest time to visit is for the **Carnival** held over **Christmas** and the

New Year. **J'Ouvert** is on Boxing Day with dancing through the streets of Basseterre, with parades on New Year's Day, followed by calypso competitions and festivities going on until the beginning of Feb. It is a favourite time of year for many Kittitians and Nevisians with never a dull moment. For details, contact the Ministry of Culture, www.stkittscarnival.com.

Nevis
Jan Carnival.
Apr The annual 4-km **Nevis to St Kitts Cross Channel Swim**.
Jul-Aug The annual equivalent of carnival is **Culturama**, held end Jul and finishing on the 1st Mon in Aug. There is a Queen show, calypso competition, local bands and guest bands and 'street jams'. The Nevis Tourist Office has full details or contact the Department of Culture, T869-469 5521, Mon-Fri 0800-1600.
Sep **Nevis Running Festival** incorporates a marathon, half marathon and shorter distances of 10 km and 5 km. Contact the **Nevis Cycle & Triathlon Club**, T869-662 3975, www.neviscycleclub.com.
Nov Nevis hosts an **international triathlon** comprising a 2-km swim, 90-km bike ride and 21-km run, followed by a beach bash, T869-469 9682, www.nevistriathlon.com.

Literature

Three island-born novelists stand out as eminent in their field with worldwide respect for their work, none of whom now lives in the islands. **EA Markham** was born in Montserrat in 1939 and moved to Britain to study in 1956. He has since lived in various countries all round the world working as a theatre director and a magazine editor, while also writing short stories, plays, a travel book and six collections of his poetry. Despite his international career and many years living in the UK, his childhood memories of Montserrat are a recurring topic in his work.

Jamaica Kincaid was born in St John's, Antigua, in 1949 as Elaine Potter Richardson. As a young woman she moved to the USA to work as a children's nanny, later becoming a journalist and author. Many visitors regard Antigua as the ideal Caribbean holiday destination. The role of tourism in Antigua is, however, one of the objects of a vehement attack in Jamaica Kincaid's first book, *A Small Place*. Addressed to the foreign visitor, the essay proposes to reveal the realities underneath the island's surface. What follows is a passionate indictment of much of Antiguan government, society, the colonists who laid its foundations and the modern tourist. It is a profoundly negative book, designed to inspire the visitor to think beyond the beach and the hotel on this, or any other, island. Memories and images from her childhood, together with the problems of race and gender faced by black women, figure strongly in her other books to date, including *Annie John* (1985), *Lucy* (1990) and *Autobiography of My Mother* (1996).

Caryl Phillips was born in St Kitts in 1958 but brought up in Leeds and educated at Oxford University. He has a prolific output of screenplays, radio and theatre plays, fiction and non-fiction. His novels reflect the West Indian concern with alienation and isolation and deal with slavery, emigration, poverty and longing. *Crossing the River*, about slavery and the African diaspora, was shortlisted for the Booker Prize in 1993.

Essentials A-Z

Accident and emergency

Antigua and Barbuda
T911 or T999.

Montserrat
Police T999. Fire T911. Glendon Hospital, T664-491 2552/7404.

St Kitts and Nevis
Police/ambulance T911. Fire T333 (St Kitts), T869-469 3444 (Nevis).

Children

All kids love the beach and there is no shortage of beaches in the Leeward Islands. Antigua and St Kitts are good starting points with direct flights from London, Canada and the USA, making the transatlantic journey less stressful. However, most children will delight in taking a small plane to one of the neighbouring islands and a 2-centre holiday should not be dismissed. The islands are small, so if you hire a car children will not have time to get bored before reaching their destination. There are not many historical sites and few museums to drag them around, but those that exist are often related to pirates and sea battles to excite the imagination. Day sails on catamarans are always popular for older children and there are lots of opportunities for them to learn to windsurf, sail or take part in other watersports. Most of the hotels can arrange babysitters for small

children and some of the larger resorts have kids' clubs.

Departure tax

Antigua and Barbuda
Airport departure charges are included in all tickets.

Montserrat
EC$35 (US$13) for Caricom residents and EC$55 (US$21) for visitors.

St Kitts and Nevis
There is an airport departure tax of EC$60 (US$22) per person payable in cash or crédit card from St Kitts, EC$54 (US$20.50) from Nevis.

Electricity

Antigua and Barbuda
220/110 volts; check before using your own appliances. Many hotels have transformers.

Montserrat
220/110 volts, 60 cycles.

St Kitts and Nevis
230 volts AC/60 cycles (some hotels have 110 volts).

Embassies and consulates

For a full list of embassies and consulates see http://embassy.goabroad.com.

Health

See your GP or travel clinic at least 6 weeks before departure for general advice on travel risks and vaccinations. Try phoning a specialist travel clinic if your own doctor is unfamiliar with health in the region. Make sure you have sufficient medical travel insurance, get a dental check, know your own blood group and if you suffer a long-term condition such as diabetes or epilepsy, obtain a Medic Alert bracelet/necklace (www.medicalert.org.uk). If you wear glasses, take a copy of your prescription.

Vaccinations

It is important to confirm your primary courses and boosters are up to date. It is also advisable to vaccinate against **tetanus**, **typhoid** and **hepatitis A**. Vaccines sometimes advised are **hepatitis B**, **rabies** and **diphtheria**. **Yellow fever** vaccination is not required unless you are coming directly from an infected country in Africa or South America. Although the **cholera** vaccination is largely ineffective, immigration officers may ask for proof that you've had it if coming from a country where an epidemic has occurred. Check www.who.int for updates. **Malaria** is not a danger in these islands.

Health risks

The most common affliction of travellers to any country is probably **diarrhoea** and the same is true of the Leeward Islands. Tap water is safe to drink in hotels and resorts, but bottled water is widely available. Swimming in sea or river water that has been contaminated by sewage can be a cause of diarrhoea; ask locally if it is safe. Diarrhoea may also be caused by viruses, bacteria (such as E-coli), protozoal (such as giardia), salmonella and cholera. It may be accompanied by vomiting or by severe abdominal pain. Any kind of diarrhoea responds well to the replacement of water and salts. Sachets of rehydration salts can be bought in most chemists and can be dissolved in boiled water. If the symptoms persist, consult a doctor.

There is no malaria but there is a risk of dengue fever and chikungunya (also known as chik V) and there are lots of mosquitoes at certain times of the year, so take insect repellent and avoid being bitten as much as possible. **Dengue fever** and chikungunya are particularly hard to protect against as the mosquitoes can bite throughout the day as well as night (unlike those that carry malaria). **Chikungunya virus** is relatively new in the Caribbean and is spreading through the islands. Sleep off the ground under a mosquito net and use some kind of insecticide. Remember that DEET (Di-ethyltoluamide) is the gold standard. Apply the repellent every 4-6 hrs but more often if you are sweating heavily. If a non-DEET product is used, check who tested it. Validated products (tested at the London School of Hygiene and Tropical Medicine) include Mosiguard, non-DEET Jungle formula and non-DEET Autan. If you want to use citronella remember that it must be applied very frequently (ie hourly) to be effective.

Tiny sandflies, known locally as 'noseeums' often appear on the beaches in the late afternoon and can give nasty stings. Keep a good supply of repellent and make sure you wash off all sand to avoid taking them with you from the beach. Do not eat the little green apples of the manchineel tree, as they are poisonous, and don't sit under the tree in the rain as the dripping oil from the leaves causes blisters. Some beaches, particularly those on the west coast, get jellyfish at certain times of the year, for example Jul/Aug.

The climate is hot; the islands are tropical and protection against the sun will be needed. Do not be deceived by cooling sea breezes. To reduce the risk of **sunburn** and skin cancer, make sure you pack high-factor sun cream, loose clothing (light colours are cooler) and a hat.

If you get sick

There are hospitals, medical centres and clinics, while the larger hotels have doctors on call. The nearest hyperbaric chambers are on Saba and St Thomas. Make sure you have adequate insurance (see below). Remember you cannot dial any toll-free numbers abroad so make sure you have a contact number.

Useful websites

www.bgtha.org British Global and Travel Health Association.
www.cdc.gov Centers for Disease Control and Prevention;

US government site that gives excellent advice on travel health and details of disease outbreaks.
www.fco.gov.uk British Foreign and Commonwealth Office travel site has useful information on each country, people, climate and a list of UK embassies/consulates.
www.fitfortravel.scot.nhs.uk A-Z of vaccine/health advice for each country.
www.sensitivescreening.com/ mht.htm Number One Health Group offers travel screening services, vaccine and travel health advice, email/SMS text vaccine reminders and screens returned travellers for tropical diseases.

Insurance

All travellers should obtain comprehensive insurance including medical insurance. Insurance should be valid for the full duration of your stay and should cover medical evacuation. You should check any exclusions and that your policy covers you for all the activities you want to undertake, such as scuba diving or horse riding.

Language

English is the official language.

Money

The currency is the East Caribbean dollar, EC$. The exchange rate is fixed at EC$2.70=US$1, but there are variations depending on where you change your money. US and Canadian dollars are widely accepted. All major credit cards and TCs are accepted.

Credit cards, currency cards and ATMs

Credit cards are widely used and ATMs can be found at banks in all the main towns. However, cafés, rum shops and small operators only accept cash. Keep your money, credit cards, etc, either safely on your person, or in a hotel safe. If your guesthouse has no safe in which to store money, passport, tickets, etc, try a local bank.

Some people recommend setting up 2 bank accounts before travelling. One has all your funds but no debit card; the other has no funds but does have a debit card. As you travel, use the internet to transfer money from the full account to the empty account when you need it and withdraw cash from an ATM. That way, if your debit card is stolen, you won't be at risk of losing all your capital. Also, by using a debit card rather than a credit card you incur fewer bank charges.

Another alternative is to take a pre-paid currency card. They look like a credit or debit card and are issued by specialist money-changing companies, such as **Travelex**, **Caxton FX** or the **Post Office**. You can top up and check your balance by phone, online and sometimes by text.

Exchange

There are banks in St John's, Basseterre and Charlestown and a couple of banks on Montserrat where you can exchange foreign currencies. However, if travelling to Barbuda, take sufficient EC$ cash. In general, the US dollar is the best currency to take, as cash or traveller's cheques. The latter are convenient and can be replaced if lost or stolen. Euros and sterling can be exchanged without difficulty but at a poor rate, and US dollars are preferred.

Cost of living

The islands are expensive, reflecting the need to import most daily essential items and the lack of any economies of scale. High season is Dec-Apr, when hotel prices are at their highest. Good deals can be found in hurricane season, particularly Sep-Nov. Cheap and cheerful lodging can be found for US$40-50 a night, but it will not be on the beach. Generally, a room in a decent hotel or guesthouse will cost in the region of US$100 a night, or more for the luxury places. Some of the cheaper accommodation can only be reached with a rental car. Renting a house or apartment is an option for a group so you can share the cost. Eating in local cafeterias, drinking in rum shops and travelling on buses can save you money.

Opening hours

Antigua and Barbuda

Banks Mon-Thu 0800-1400; Fri 0800-1200, 1400-1600. Bank of Antigua opens Sat 0800-1200.
Shops Mon-Sat 0800-1200, 1300-1700, although Thu and Sat are early closing days for some non-tourist shops. On Sun most places close, though the supermarkets at Woods Centre, English Harbour and Jolly Harbour open all day and shops in St John's will open if there is a cruise ship in port.

Montserrat

Government offices Mon-Fri 0800-1600. **Shops** 0800-1600, but early closing Wed and Sat afternoons.

St Kitts and Nevis

Government offices Mon-Fri 0900-1600. **Shops** Mon-Sat 0800-1600, some open on Sun if a cruise ship is in port. Early closing Thu and also Sat for some shops.

Public holidays

Antigua and Barbuda

New Year's Day (1 Jan), **Good Fri**, **Easter Mon**, **Labour Day** (1st Mon in May), **Whit Mon** (end May), **Independence Day** (1 Nov), **National Heroes Day** (9 Dec), **Christmas Day** (25 Dec) and **Boxing Day** (26 Dec).

Montserrat

New Year's Day, **St Patrick's Day** (17 Mar), **Good Fri**, **Easter Mon**, **Labour Day** (1st Mon in May), **Whit Mon** (7th Mon after Easter), **Queen's birthday** (middle Mon in Jun), **Aug Mon** (1st Mon in Aug), **Christmas Day** (25 Dec), **Boxing Day** (26 Dec).

St Kitts and Nevis

New Year's Day (1 Jan), **Carnival Day/Las' Lap** (2 Jan), **Good Fri**, **Easter Mon**, **Labour Day** (1st Mon in May), **Whit Mon** (end May), **Aug Mon/Emancipation Day** (beginning of Aug), **National Heroes Day** (16 Sep), **Independence Day** (19 Sep), **Christmas Day** (25 Dec), **Boxing Day** (26 Dec).

Safety

The Caribbean is a relatively safe part of the world in which to travel. The visitor usually only needs to worry about petty theft such as bag snatching on the beach. Always report such incidents to the police. Do not leave your possessions unattended on the beach; leave valuables in the hotel safe and, if renting a car, keep everything out of sight and locked in the boot. Don't offer lifts to strangers. Street lighting is patchy so avoid dark streets at night. Do not go to out-of-the-way or deserted beaches at night and do not sleep on the beach. There has been an increase of gun crime on Antigua and St Kitts in recent years. For the latest advice contact the British FCO or the US travel advisory services.

Note that the penalties for possession of narcotics are very severe and no mercy is shown towards tourists.

Telephone

The international code for Antigua and Barbuda is 268, for Montserrat 664 and for St Kitts and Nevis 869. Landline and mobile services are provided by **LIME** (www.lime.com), while **Digicel** (www.digicelgroup.com) also provide mobile services on Antigua and Barbuda and St Kitts and Nevis. Before you leave home check with your mobile or smart phone provider will work in the island you are visiting. With the right phone most apps should be accessible. Internet phone services are also available, but note that resorts often charge for Wi-Fi. It is also possible to buy or rent a mobile phone, or buy a local SIM card to put in your own phone (it must be unlocked).

Time

Atlantic standard time, 4 hrs behind GMT, 1 hr ahead of EST.

Tipping

Tipping is recommended. You should usually tip in restaurants, even if a service charge is added to the bill, and also leave a tip for the person who has cleaned your hotel room. Tip taxi drivers; porters usually expect US$1-2 per bag. Guides and other staff on day trips welcome tips and often have a pot to put them in.

Tourist information

Each country has its own websites, see below, and Facebook pages for latest news and events. In addition, the **Caribbean Tourism Organization** (**CTO**) has an umbrella site with links to individual islands: www.onecaribbean.org.

Antigua and Barbuda

Antigua Tourist Office, ACB Financial Centre, High St, St John's, T268-562 7600, www.antigua-barbuda.org. Mon-Fri 0830-1600, Sat 0830-1200. Gives list of official taxi charges and hotel information. Barbuda has a Tourism Department here, too. The Antigua Tourist Office at the airport helps book accommodation mainly at the more expensive resorts. Also

useful is the **Antigua Hotels and Tourist Association**, Island House, Newgate St, St John's, T268-462 0374, www.antiguahotels.org. In addition, there is a wealth of information on www.antiguanice.com and the authoritative source of information on Barbuda is www.barbudaful.net.

Montserrat

Montserrat Tourist Board, Upstairs the Public Market, Little Bay, T664-491 2230, www.visitmontserrat.com.

St Kitts and Nevis

St Kitts Tourism Authority, Pelican Mall, Basseterre, T869-465 4040, www.stkittstourism.kn, Mon-Fri 0800-1600.
Nevis Tourism Authority, Old Treasury Building, Main St, Charlestown, T869-469 7550, www.nevisisland.com, Mon-Fri 0800-1700. Both are extremely helpful, with plenty of information available.

Visas and immigration

Since the clampdown on security in 2006/2007, all travellers need a passport to travel to or from the Caribbean. On all forms, refer to yourself as a 'visitor' rather than a 'tourist'. If asked where you are staying and you have not booked in advance, say any hotel (they do not usually check), but do not say that you are going to arrange accommodation later. You should carry your passport in a safe place about your person, or if not going far, leave it in the hotel safe. It is also a good idea to keep photocopies of essential documents, as well as additional passport-sized photographs.

Antigua and Barbuda
A valid passport and onward ticket only are required by UK, US and Canadian citizens, nationals of Commonwealth countries (except for Bangladesh, Cameroon, The Gambia, Ghana, India, Mozambique, Nigeria, Pakistan, Sierra Leone and Sri Lanka), British Dependent Territories, citizens of EU countries and most of Latin America and the Caribbean and many other countries if their stay does not exceed 6 months. Those in transit or visiting from a cruise ship for less than 24 hrs don't need visas. Visitors must also prove that they have enough money for their stay, and provide an address (even a temporary one).

Montserrat
A valid passport is required except for US, Canadian and British visitors, who must only show proof of citizenship for stays of up to 6 months. However, US citizens will need a passport to re-enter the USA. Citizens of Caricom countries may travel with their official ID card. Visas, which may be required for visitors from Haiti and Cuba, can be obtained from British consulate offices. An onward or return ticket is required.

St Kitts and Nevis
OECS nationals need a driver's licence or birth certificate. Other nationalities need passports and a return ticket, but for up to 6 months visas are not required for Commonwealth and EU countries and nationals of member countries of the OAS, with the exception of the Dominican Republic and Haiti.

Weights and measures

Imperial.

Contents

Footprint features

Antigua & Barbuda

Antigua, covering about 108 sq miles, is the largest of the Leeward Islands, and also one of the most popular. Its dependencies are nearby Barbuda and Redonda. The island is low-lying and composed of volcanic rock, coral and limestone. There is nothing spectacular about its landscape, although the rolling hills and flowering trees are pretty. The coastline however, curving into coves and graceful harbours with 365 soft white-sand beaches fringed with palm trees, is among the most attractive in the West Indies. English Harbour is particularly picturesque, with yachts filling a historic bay that has been a popular staging post for centuries. Nelson's Dockyard and ruined forts are overlooked by the old battery on Shirley Heights, now better known for Sunday jump-ups, reggae and steel bands. Some 30 miles to the north of Antigua, the remote coral island of Barbuda is attractive for hikers, nature lovers, cyclists and beachcombers. Direct, non-stop flights from Europe and North America together with great beaches, watersports and safe swimming make Antigua ideal for introducing children to the Caribbean.

Wildlife on Antigua and Barbuda

Around 150 different birds have been observed on Antigua and Barbuda, of which a third are year-round residents and the rest seasonal or migrants. Good spots for birdwatching include Potworks Dam, noted for the great blue heron in spring and many water fowl. Great Bird Island is home to the red-billed tropic bird and on Man of War Island, Barbuda, frigate birds breed. The Antiguan Racer Conservation Project was set up in 1995 to save the harmless Antiguan racer snake (*Alsophis antiguae*) which had been devastated by mongooses and black rats. The 60 remaining snakes were all on Great Bird Island and a campaign to eliminate the rats here and on other offshore islands helped their numbers to increase, together with other rare wildlife. Racers have now been reintroduced to other islands.

Arriving in Antigua

Getting there

Antigua has excellent connections by air with Europe and North America as well as with neighbouring islands such as Guadeloupe, Dominica or Sint Maarten in addition to the other Leeward islands included in this book, making Antigua ideal for a two-centre holiday or the starting point for more protracted island hopping. It is not easy to get there by sea, other than on a cruise ship or private yacht, as there are no formal ferry links except to the sister island of Barbuda and to Montserrat. ▸▸ *See Transport, page 57.*

Getting around

Renting a **car** is probably the best way to see the island's sights, as the bus service is inadequate, but be aware that roads are very bumpy and narrow and speed bumps are poorly marked. Finding your way around is not easy; there are no road signs and street names are rarely in evidence. **Cycling** is possible but not very interesting for adventurous cyclists. There are car hire companies in St John's and some at the airport, most will pick you up. Be careful with one-way streets in St John's. At night people do not always dim their headlights and watch out for pedestrians. **Minivans** (shared taxis) go to some parts of the island (for example Old Road) from the West End bus terminal by the market in St John's. **Buses** serve the southern part of the island but not the north, so there are no buses to the airport.

Built around the largest of the natural harbours is St John's, the capital, formerly guarded by Fort Barrington and Fort James either side of the entrance to the harbour. The town is a mixture of the old and the new, with a few historical sights. Some of the old buildings in St John's, including the **Anglican cathedral** ① *Newgate St and Long St, donations requested*, have been damaged several times by earthquakes, most recently in 1974. A cathedral in St John's was first built in 1683, but replaced in 1745 and then again in 1843 after an earthquake, at which time it was built of stone. Its twin towers can be seen from all over St John's. It has a wonderfully cool interior lined with pitch pine timber. The **Antigua Recreation Ground** alongside the cathedral contains what was the main cricket pitch, used for Test matches, but this was replaced by a new ground for the 2007 Cricket World Cup. There are still some run-down parts but the cruise ship docks area has been developed for tourism: boutiques,

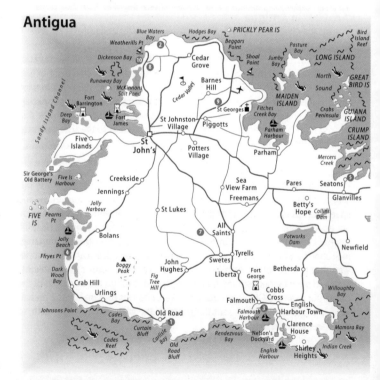

Antigua

duty-free shops and restaurants compete for custom. Most activity now takes place around the two quay developments: **Redcliff Quay** is a picturesque area of restored historical buildings now full of boutiques, souvenir shops, bars and cafés; **Heritage Quay** is a duty-free shopping complex with a casino, strategically placed to catch cruise ship visitors. When a cruise ship is in dock many passengers come ashore and it becomes very crowded. There is a vendors' mall next to Heritage Quay, selling souvenirs.

The **Museum of Antigua and Barbuda** ① *Long St, T268-462 4930, www.antiguamuseums.net, Mon-Fri 0830-1630, Sat 1000-1400, free (donations requested)*, at the former courthouse is worth a visit, both to see the exhibitions of anthropology of Antigua, pre-Columbian and colonial archaeology, and for the courthouse building itself, believed to be the oldest building in town. First erected in 1750, damaged by earthquakes in 1843 and 1974, it originally housed the Court of Justice on the ground floor and meeting rooms for the Legislative Council and Assembly upstairs. Cricket fans will be pleased to see Viv Richards' cricket bat, with which he scored the fastest century, among the more recent exhibits. The **Historical and Archaeological Society of Antigua and Barbuda (HAS)** which manages the museum publishes an interesting newsletter. It also organizes field trips. The **Environment Awareness Group** is also here and there's an interesting gift shop with locally made items.

Where to stay 🛏
Blue Waters **2**
Carlisle Bay **1**
Catamaran **3**
Coco's Antigua **4**
Ellen Bay Inn **5**
Nonsuch Bay Resort **6**
Paige Pond
　Country Inn **7**
Siboney Beach Club **10**
Tree Tops Cottage **11**
Villas at Sunset Lane **8**
Wind Chimes Inn **9**

The northwest and north
→ *For listings, see pages 43-59.*

This is a popular area for a beach holiday with a long stretch of hotels, restaurants, bars and nightlife, plenty of watersports and easy access to the Cedar Valley Golf Course. St John's is a few minutes away by taxi. Dickenson Bay and Runaway Bay are the two main beaches, separated from the main road by McKinnons Salt Pond. Windsurfing and kitesurfing are good off the coast north of the airport.

At the north side of the entrance to St John's harbour are the ruins of **Fort James**, from where you can get a good view of St John's. There was originally a fort on this site dating from 1675, but most now dates from 1749. In the second half of the 18th century there were 36 guns and barracks for 75 soldiers. In the 19th century a gun was fired at sunrise, sunset and to salute visiting warships. The ruins are sorely neglected and in dire need of attention and preservation. To get there, head north out of St John's, turn west to the sea, then follow the road parallel to the beach to the end. There is a lovely beach here and the area is popular with Antiguans at weekends when they come to 'lime', eat at the beach bar, play beach cricket or volleyball and listen to live music. There is not much of historical interest to see, except the 1805 cannon but the views are lovely. Some horse riding tours and segway tours include it on their routes and cruise ship passengers are brought to the beach here as it

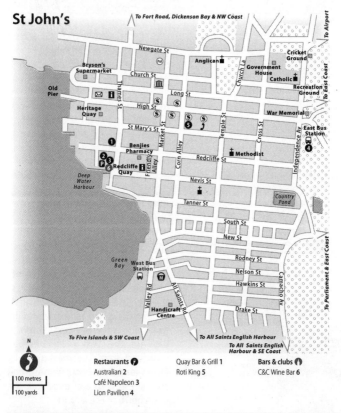

St John's

Restaurants 🍴
Australian 2
Café Napoleon 3
Lion Pavilion 4

Quay Bar & Grill 1
Roti King 5

Bars & clubs 🍸
C&C Wine Bar 6

is so close to the port. At times the sea can be rough and then turns milky in appearance with lots of weed – not good for swimming.

Further north, but better, are **Dickenson Bay** and **Runaway Bay**, adjacent long stretches of white sand, separated by a small promontory. Dickenson Bay is wall-to-wall, low-rise hotels, with watersports outlets, bars and restaurants on the beach. The sea is calm and perfect for children, with roped off areas to ensure safety from motor craft. Much of the southern beach has been eroded by storms and there are some ruined beach houses at that end. **Soldier's Bay**, next to the **Blue Waters** hotel; is shallow and picturesque. Also good is **Deep Bay** which, like most beaches, can only be reached by taxi or car.

The north coast is ideal for windsurfing and kitesurfing. **Dutchman's Bay** has been a windsurfing mecca for decades, but kitesurfing was initially banned because of the proximity of the airport. **Jabberwock Beach** is now 'kite beach' and conditions are excellent with cross-onshore winds, a long sandy beach and shallow water. The best season is January-July when winds are in the 20-knot range.

The west → *For listings, see pages 43-59.*

West of St John's are the ruins of **Fort Barrington**, on a promontory at Goat Hill overlooking Deep Bay and the entrance to St John's Harbour. It was erected by Governor Burt, who gave up active duty in 1780 suffering from psychiatric disorders; a stone he placed in one of the walls at the fort describes him grandly as 'Imperator and Gubernator' of the Carib Islands. The previous fortifications saw the most action in Antigua's history, with the French and English battling for possession in the 17th century. Today there is not much to see of the fort as it has not been restored and is overgrown, but it is a good walk up the hill and you get a wonderful view of St John's harbour on one side and Deep Bay on the other. It's a bit of a scramble in places so wear trainers or proper shoes.

There are several nice beaches on the peninsula west of St John's. On **Trafalgar Beach** condominiums have been built on the rocks overlooking the small, sheltered bay. If you go through **Five Islands** village you come to **Galley Bay**, a secluded and unspoilt hotel beach which is popular with locals and joggers at sunset. The four **Hawksbill** beaches at the end of the peninsula are crescent shaped, very scenic and unspoilt. Hotel guests tend to use the second beach, leaving the other three empty. Take drinks to the furthest one (clothes optional, secluded and pleasant) as there are no facilities and you may have the place to yourself.

Heading south from St John's, you pass the marina at **Jolly Harbour**, where there is a beach and large hotel development, before reaching **Dark Wood Beach** and **Cades Bay** on the road to Old Road round the southwest coast. Darkwood has beautiful white sand and is comparatively empty as there is no hotel here. Looking out across the turquoise sea you get a good view of Montserrat. Both have a beach bar serving cold beer and food with decent toilets and plenty of parking. Offshore, the 2½-mile **Cades Reef** is popular with snorkellers and divers. Inland you can see the black pineapple being grown at the Cades Bay Agricultural Station.

Fig Tree Drive between Old Road and the Catholic church on the road going north from Liberta, is a steep, winding road, through mountainous rainforest. If travelling by bicycle make sure you go *down* Fig Tree Drive from the All Saints to Liberta road, heading towards Old Road; the hill is very steep. It is greener and more scenic than most of the island, but the rainforest is scanty and incomparable with islands like Dominica. It does, however, give you a good idea of what Antigua must have looked like before the land was cleared for sugar and you can see banana plants, mango and breadfruit trees as well as the pineapple farm. There are no figs; the name comes from the local name for the green banana, which is green fig. There are roadside booths where you can try whatever fruit is in season, which is amazingly sweet and tasty. **Fig Tree Studio Art Gallery** ① *T268-460 1234, www.figtreestudioart.com, Mon-Sat 0930-1730 Nov-Jun*, is an interesting place to stop, showcasing the work of Sallie Harker (www.sallieharker.com) and lots of local and regional art and crafts. Another local attraction is **Antigua Rainforest Zipline Tours** ① *Fig Tree Drive, Wallings, T268-562 6363, http://antiguarainforest.com, US$69-79*, to give you a bit of an adrenaline rush. It's a popular activity for cruise passengers and families with older children. Day trips with other excursions or activities added on (such as kayaking or a beach) can also be arranged.

Boggy Peak, renamed Mount Obama in 2009, in the southwest, is the highest point on the island and from the top you can get wonderful views over to Guadeloupe, St Kitts, Nevis and Montserrat. It is a good walk up, or you can take a car but the road is very steep and only partly paved, so 4WD is best, but even that is very hard work up and down and you may have no tread left on your tyres afterwards. From Urlings, walk (or take a minibus) just over half a mile in the direction of Old Town. There is a clear track on the left (ask the bus driver to drop you off there) which is very straight then ascends quite steeply. When you get to the top, walk round the fence surrounding the communications tower to get a good view in all directions. It takes over an hour to walk up and you are advised not to wander around alone.

The southeast is the area of most historical interest, with the old naval dockyard which was of such strategic importance in the 17th and 18th centuries. Now a leading marina, it is a mecca for yachts from all over the world and many world-class yacht races are held here. Yachtsmen and women need entertainment and there are several good hotels, lots of restaurants, bars and nightlife in both Falmouth Harbour and English Harbour, which are also the best places to arrange a wide range of watersports. Former military buildings dot the hillsides up to the top of Shirley Heights, from where you get a spectacular view of the coastline, popular with visitors on Sunday for a barbecue, steel band and reggae.

English Harbour and Nelson's Dockyard
ⓘ *US$8 entrance to the Dockyard (guided tour), the Interpretation Centre (guided tour), the Block House and Shirley Heights, children under 12 free. Souvenirs and t-shirts are on sale at the entrance. National Parks Antigua, T268-481 5028, http://nationalparksantigua.com.*

On the other side of the island from St John's is **English Harbour**, which has become one of the world's most attractive yachting centres and is now a 'hot spot' at night for tourists. Here Nelson's Dockyard, the hub of English maritime power in the region, has been restored and is one of the most interesting

English Harbour & Shirley Heights

| 20 metres | Where to stay 🛏 | Anchorage Rooms 2 | Ocean Inn 5 |
| 20 yards | Admiral's Inn 1 | Galleon Beach 3 | |

historical monuments in the West Indies. It is the only existing Georgian Naval Dockyard in the world and was designated a national park in 1985. Nelson served in Antigua as a young man for almost three years, and visited it again in 1805, during his long chase of Villeneuve which was to end with the Battle of Trafalgar. The film *Longitude*, starring Jeremy Irons, was filmed here, standing in for Jamaica and Barbados. The **Nelson's Dockyard Museum** has been renovated to provide a complete history of this famous Georgian Naval Dockyard and the story of famous English Harbour. **Admiral's Inn**, with its boat and mast yard, slipway and pillars still standing, suffered earthquake damage in the 19th century. The **Copper and Lumber Store** is now a hotel, bar and restaurant. On the quay are three large capstans, showing signs of wear and tear. Boat charters can be arranged from here. A footpath leads round the bay to **Fort Berkeley** at the harbour mouth, well grazed by goats, and wonderful views. Near the dockyard, **Clarence House** still stands where the future King of England, William IV, stayed when he served as a midshipman.

On the left of the road from English Harbour to Shirley Heights are the remains of the British Navy's magazines and a small branch road to the **Dow Hill Interpretation Centre**, which offers an interesting 15-minute multimedia show every 15 minutes on the history of the island. There is a gift shop, restaurant and small museum with shell display. Local guides are also available.

At **Shirley Heights**, overlooking English Harbour, are the ruins of fortifications built in the 18th century, with a wonderful view. Some buildings, such as officers' quarters, are still standing, restored but roofless, giving an idea of their former grandeur. At the lookout point, or **Battery**, at the south end is a bar and restaurant. On Sunday a steel band plays 1600-1900, followed by reggae 1900-2200, very loud and popular. There are barbecued burgers, chicken, ribs and salad available. It is usually full of tourists, often packed, and later on the crowd can be drunk and rowdy. **Great George Fort**, on Monk's Hill, above Falmouth Harbour (a 30-minute walk from the village of Liberta, and from Cobb's Cross near English Harbour) is less well preserved.

Near English Harbour is **Galleon Beach**, which is splendid, and you can get a water taxi from English Harbour. It has an excellent hotel and restaurant. There is a cave on **Windward Beach**, near English Harbour, which is good for a moonlight bonfire (go in a group, not just as a couple). Follow the road past the Antigua Yacht Club leading to Pigeon Beach and turn left to Windward Beach on a bumpy track, best with a 4WD.

Rendezvous Bay West of Falmouth Harbour is the glorious Rendezvous Bay, a long, curved bay backed by steep hills and forest, until recently accessible only by a hiking trail (even 4WD vehicles get stuck), horse (from nearby Spring Hill Riding Stables) or by boat. It is part of the 5000-acre national park surrounding English Harbour. However, in 2014 work started on construction of a low-density, luxury hotel and villa development and an access road was to be cut from the main Falmouth road.

Half Moon Bay At Half Moon Bay, in the east, there is plenty of room on a lovely long, curved, white-sand beach; the waves can be rough in the centre of the bay, but the water is calm at the north end where there are also trees for shade and you can snorkel. One of the most beautiful bays on the island, if not the most beautiful, it has something for everyone, with rock pools to entertain children, beach loungers for rent for sun worshippers and surf for active types. The hotel on the south side of the bay is long abandoned and hurricane-damaged, but interesting to explore. A snack bar serves cold drinks and ice cream, but does not open regular hours, while vendors ply their wares in the car park.

The northeast and islands offshore → For listings, see pages 43-59.

Parham is the site of the first settlement on the island and the area is full of secluded bays offering safe harbour for shipping, shielded by numerous islands offshore, now either protected as nature reserves or used as exclusive resorts for the wealthy. You can go kayaking in the mangroves or visit the stingrays kept in a shallow area at the mouth of a bay off Seatons. Evidence of past dependence on sugar can be seen by visiting Betty's Hope, where the mill has been restored and opened to visitors. Good spots for birdwatching include **Potworks Dam** a little further south, noted for the great blue heron in spring and many waterfowl. **Harmony Hall** (see page 47) is an excellent place for lunch and a visit to the art gallery. A car is essential for visiting the villages in the northeast and east, as there are no buses.

If you have a car, try taking the road out to the airport from St John's, now called the Sir George H Walter Highway. Do not enter the airport, but take the right fork which runs alongside it. After about 1½ miles take a right turn down a small road to **St George's Church**, on **Fitches Creek Bay**, built in 1687 in a beautiful location, and with interesting gravestones, including the marble tombstone of the first English settler to be buried within a place of worship in 1659. It was remodeled in 1735. From here, a rough coast road leads to **Parham**, which was the first British settlement on the island and has an attractive and unusual octagonal church, **St Peter's**, which dates from the 1840s, surrounded by flamboyant trees. Designed by Thomas Weekes in the Palladian style, it dates from the 1840s. Parham was once the main port, exporting sugar from some 20 sugar estates, but after 1920 it ceased to be a port of entry and its fortunes declined along with those of sugar. On Market Street are the remains of imposing Georgian buildings.

From Parham go due south and then east at the petrol station through Pares to **Willikies**. On this road, just past Pares village, is a sign to **Betty's Hope** ⓘ *visitor centre Mon and Wed-Sat 0830-1600, for a guided tour contact the Museum of Antigua and Barbuda (see page 31), T268-462 4930*, a ruined sugar estate built in 1650 and owned by the Codrington family 1674-1944. Restoration was carried out by the Museum of Antigua and Barbuda in St John's and it was officially opened in 1995. One of the twin windmills can sometimes be seen working. The visitor centre tells the story of life on a sugar plantation and is well worth a visit. Sir Christopher Codrington established the first large sugar estate in Antigua in 1674 and leased Barbuda to raise provisions for his plantations. Forests were cleared for sugar cane production and slave labour was imported. Today many Antiguans blame frequent droughts on the island's lack of trees to attract rainfall, and ruined mill towers of sugar plantations stand as testament to the barrenness.

At **Seatons**, you can get a boat out into a shallow area at the edge of a bay to what is known as **Sting Ray City** ⓘ *T268-562 7297, www.stingraycityantigua. com, US$50*. Southern stingrays are confined in a large pen on a sandbank in the sea (there are also a few huge starfish). If you take a tour, you are given snorkelling gear to get into the water with the rays, which come up to be fed. You can hold them under the water; they are quite harmless.

After Willikies the road is signed to the **Pineapple Beach Club** at **Long Bay**, but before you get there, take a right turn down a small road, which deteriorates to a bumpy track, to **Devil's Bridge** at Indian Town Point (look for signs for the Verandah). The area on the Atlantic coast is a national park where rough waves have carved out the bridge and made blowholes, not easily visible at first, but quite impressive when the spray breaks through. It is said that African slaves from the nearby plantations threw themselves off the bridge in desperation, with locals saying 'the devil made them do it'. There's a good view of Long Bay and the headland.

Long Island Offshore, Long Island is occupied by the upmarket all-inclusive hotel, **Jumby Bay**, a 300-acre property run by Rosewood Hotels for those who like to be pampered. At Pasture Bay, on the north side of the island, the hawksbill turtle lays its eggs from June to October. The **Environmental Awareness Group** (EAG) organizes **turtle watches** ⓘ *T268-462 6236, http://www.eagantigua.org/ page571.html, US$50 for non-members, US$45 for children*, every Friday from 1900 with 2½ hours of beach patrol. There are also turtle watches on Antigua every Saturday. Nesting season is approximately June-October.

Great Bird Island This 20-acre islet just off the northeast coast of Antigua is part of the North Sound National Park. It got its name when sailors noticed that an extraordinary number of birds lived on the island and there are still colonies of red-billed tropic birds, West Indian whistling ducks, brown pelicans and magnificent frigate birds. However, the island is most important as being the last remaining habitat for the harmless Antiguan racer snake (*Alsophis antiguae*). The Antiguan Racer Conservation Project was set up in 1995 to save the population of snakes, which had been devastated by mongooses and rats (see box, page 29). The 60 remaining snakes were helped by a predator-elimination drive and numbers have increased. Boat parties come here for the two pristine beaches on the island and the mangroves and reef offer some of the best snorkelling around Antigua.

Barbuda → *For listings, see pages 43-59.*

Some 30 miles to the north of Antigua is Barbuda, a flat coral island 68 miles square, one of the two island dependencies of Antigua. A visit here is like going back in time: there are few paved roads, no crime and the people are friendly – life is slow and simple.

Most residents live in the only village on the island, **Codrington**, which stands on the edge of a large lagoon. Barbuda has a fascinating history, having been privately owned in colonial times by the Codrington family, who used it to supply their sugar estates on Antigua with food and slaves. This caused problems after emancipation as all property belonged to the Codringtons and the freed slaves were trapped with no jobs, no land and no laws. After many years and court cases, Antiguan law was applied to the island, but while Barbudans may own their own houses, all other land is generally held by the government. In places you can see the remains of the stone wall used to demarcate the limit of the village within which everybody had to live until 1976, when the creation of a local government inspired people to move further afield. You can also see the village well which was used to draw water until the 1980s. Tourist information can be found at **Artcafé** ① *Two Foot Bay Rd, T268-460 0434,*

Barbuda

Goat Point
GOAT IS
Hog Point
Cedar Tree Point
Codrington Lagoon
Two Feet Bay
Frigate Bird Sanctuary
Codrington
Castle Hill
Dulcina
Palmetto Point
Pelican Bay
Coco Point
Spanish Point

Where to stay
Coco Point Lodge 2
Island Chalet 3
Lighthouse Bay Resort 1
North Beach 4
Barbuda Cottages 6
Palm Tree Guesthouse 7
Nedd's Guest House 5

N

5 km
5 miles

see Facebook. Owner and artist, Claire Frank, runs this friendly café, gift shop and art gallery and is a mine of information.

This is one of the few islands in the area where there is still abundant wildlife, although much of it has been introduced by man (duck, guinea fowl, plover, pigeon, wild deer, pigs, goats, sheep, horses and donkeys), left over from the Codrington era.

There is an impressive **Frigate Bird Sanctuary** (the largest colony in the world) in the mangroves in **Codrington Lagoon**, particularly on **Man of War Island** where thousands of birds mate and breed between August and February. The sanctuary is worth a visit and the sight of 10,000 frigates raising their young is stunning (see box, opposite). Visitors are taken to only one or two spots to view the birds, and ropes keep the boats from getting too close. The rest of the birds are left entirely at peace. There are also brown boobies nesting alongside the frigates, and pelicans can be seen in the lagoon. An endemic warbler (*Dendroica subita*) lives on Barbuda and although DNA studies have been carried out, numbers and habitat requirements are so far unknown.

The **Gunchup Caves** near **Two Foot Bay** are interesting to explore. They have been have used for shelter since the days of the Amerindians. **Dark Cave** is home to a blind shrimp (*Typhlatya monae*) found only in these pools and in the Mona Island off Puerto Rico, but access is difficult. The island has a **Martello tower and fort**, the most complete historical site on the island. The tower is 56 ft high and once had nine guns to defend the southwest approach. From Codrington, River Road runs three miles to **Palmetto Point**, past Cocoa Point and on to Spanish Point, a half-mile finger of land that divides the Atlantic from the Caribbean Sea. There is a small ruin of a lookout post here and the most important Arawak settlements found in Barbuda. **Horse racing** takes place on a dirt track south of Codrington. You can sometimes see the horses being exercised around the island and taken for a swim behind a boat in the lagoon.

The beaches are an outstanding feature of Barbuda and are arguably the most magnificent in the whole Caribbean. The longest beach is a swathe of white sand stretching for 17 miles down the west side, while the most spectacular is the pink-sand beach at **Palmetto Point**, made up of zillions of tiny pink shells. There are no beach bars or vendors, you will probably be the only person for miles. There is no shade except around **Palm Beach** where a few palm trees survived past hurricane damage.

Palaster Reef is a marine reserve to protect the reef and the shipwrecks (there are around 60 ships documented and the Codringtons made a healthy income from wrecking). The seas are rich with impressive formations of elkhorn and staghorn coral, all types of crustacean and tropical fish. Lobster is plentiful and a mainstay of nearly every meal. Diving, for certified divers only, is extremely rewarding, particularly if you like exploring wrecks, but you will

Frigate birds

Fregata magnificens are indeed magnificent when seen soaring high in the air, using the thermals to suspend themselves on their huge wings for days at a time, and travel great distances. Frigates are one of the oldest known birds, with a history spanning 50 million years, and during that time they've picked up a trick or two. One of them, piracy, has earned them the nickname of man-o'-war bird. Their fishing technique relies on finding fish or squid close to the surface which they can just skim off, but failing that they have developed a method of hassling other seabirds, encouraging them to regurgitate whatever they have just caught. In an amazing display of aerobatics, the frigate birds manage to catch the food before it hits the water and get a free meal.

The breeding colony on Barbuda is believed to be the largest in the world, larger even than that of the Galápagos. Locals will tell you that there are some 10,000 birds, having recovered from the effects of Hurricane Luis in 1995, but numbers are anyone's guess. The breeding season is roughly September-January, although even later you can still see males displaying their bright red pouches, blowing them up like balloons to attract a mate. It is the male who chooses a nest site, and when he is sure he has found a long-term partner, he builds a precarious nest of twigs in the mangroves alongside all the other males. The female lays a single egg, which the male incubates and initially cares for once it is hatched. The chick is born white and fluffy and sits on the twiggy nest, suspended above the water, for eight to 10 months until it is fully fledged. It takes a lot longer to be fully proficient at flying and feeding itself.

need to take a local guide. There is no dive shop on the island but if you've got your own equipment you can hire or re-fill tanks. Snorkelling is also enjoyable.

Redonda → *For listings, see pages 43-59.*

Antigua's second dependency, 35 miles to the southwest and half a mile square, is little more than a rocky volcanic islet and is uninhabited. Columbus sighted the island on 12 November 1493 and named it after a church in Cadiz called Santa María la Redonda. He did not land, however, and thus did not formally claim the island. Neither did anyone else until 1865 when Matthew Dowdy Shiell, an Irish sea-trader from Montserrat, celebrated the birth of a long-awaited son by leading an expedition of friends to Redonda and claiming it as his kingdom. In 1872, the island was annexed by Britain and came under the jurisdiction of the colony of Antigua, despite protests from the Shiells. The title of king was not disputed, however, and has survived to this day. The island was never inhabited, although for some years guano was extracted by the Redonda Phosphate Company until the works were blown away by a hurricane.

In 1880 MD Shiell abdicated in favour of his son, Matthew Phipps Shiell, who became King Felipe of Redonda, but emigrated to the UK where he was educated and became a prolific and popular novelist. His best known novel, *The Purple Cloud* (1901), was later made into a film, *The World, the Flesh and the Devil*, starring Harry Belafonte. On his death in 1947, he appointed as his literary executor and successor to the throne his friend John Gawsworth, the poet, who became Juan, the third King of Redonda, but continued to live in London. His reign was notable for his idea of an 'intellectual aristocracy' of the realm of Redonda and he conferred titles on his literary friends, including Victor Gollancz, the publisher, JB Priestley, Dorothy L Sayers and Lawrence Durrell. This eccentric pastime hit a crisis when declining fortunes and increasing time spent in the pub sparked a rash of new titles to all and sundry, and a number of abdications in different pubs. The succession was, and still is, disputed.

The Redondan Cultural Foundation is an independent association of people interested in Redonda, its history and its monarchs, which tries to steer through the minefield of Redondan politics. It was established in 1988 by the late Reverend Paul de Fortis and exists to promote the writings of MP Shiell, John Gawsworth and other authors of the realm's 'intellectual aristocracy'. It celebrates Redonda as 'the last outpost of Bohemia'. The foundation published *The Kingdom of Redonda 1865-1990* in association with the Aylesford Press (1991).

Media interest in Redonda flares up from time to time. In May 2007, BBC Radio 4 broadcast *Redonda: The Island with too many Kings*, which included interviews with five putative monarchs. Also in 2007, a British pub, The Wellington Arms, in Southampton, tried to have itself declared an embassy of the Kingdom of Redonda in an attempt to avoid the recently introduced ban on smoking in public places.

Meanwhile, on Redonda, all is much the same for the goats, lizards and seabirds, who live an undisturbed life apart from the occasional birdwatcher who might come to find the burrowing owl, now extinct on Antigua.

◉ Antigua and Barbuda listings

For hotel and restaurant price codes and other relevant information, see pages 12-16.

◉ Where to stay

Antigua *p29, maps p30, p32 and p35*

There is a 10% service charge and 10.5% sales tax at all hotels.

$$$$ Admiral's Inn, English Harbour, T268-460 1027, www. admiralsantigua.com. This handsome Georgian brick building dating from 1788 was once a store room for pitch, turpentine and lead, while upstairs were the offices for the engineers for the Royal Naval Dockyard; the hand-hewn beams, wrought-iron chandeliers and a bar which is an old work bench scarred by the names of ships that once docked there. New suites have been added in the converted Gunpowder House on the point opposite, which also contains an art gallery. Very pleasant, excellent location, lovely views, good food in the **Pillars Restaurant** overlooking the water, live music Sat night, and at the **Boom** pool bar and restaurant at the Gunpowder House. Dinghy shuttle service around the harbour and to the Gunpowder House.

$$$$ Blue Waters, on the north coast, T268-462 0290, www.blue waters.net. One of the most upmarket on the island, with lush tropical gardens and huge mature trees on a very pretty bay. Large colonial-style rooms, suites, cottages and villas with patios or balconies, cool, clean decor with predominantly white, cream and grey colour scheme. Rates include breakfast and afternoon tea or you can opt for all-inclusive. There is a pool and watersports, a gym and tennis.

$$$$ Carlisle Bay, Old Road, T268-484 0002, www.carlisle-bay.com. Huge suites all have sea view and have been designed with dark wooden furniture, cream, white and grey furnishings and clean minimalist lines. Every luxury including offices in the rooms with wireless internet access, well-stocked minibars, restaurants and bars, a separate cinema and a library with computers. There are 9 tennis courts, 4 of which are floodlit and one has basketball hoops for children to play, pool, spa, gym, yoga and pilates, and watersports. The beach is lovely and calm in a very protected pretty bay with a view of Montserrat.

$$$$ Catamaran Hotel and Marina, Falmouth Harbour, T268-460 1036, www.catamaran-antigua.com. On a narrow man-made beach by the yachts, on a bus route or a 30-min walk to Nelson's Dockyard. 14 rooms and suites in a block on 2 floors, a/c, fans, some with TV, single or double beds, cribs for kids. Not a fancy resort, but quiet, peaceful, friendly and with a great view.

$$$$ Coco's Antigua, Jolly Harbour, T268-460 2626, www.cocoshotel.com. All-inclusive. Rooms in chattel-style wooden cottages with gingerbread fretwork, fan, fridge and a view of Jolly Beach and Five Islands. Lovely location built on a bluff with gorgeous

balconies and pleasant breeze, very romantic, restaurant, pool.
$$$$ Galleon Beach, English Harbour, T268-562 8174, www.galleon-beach-antigua.com. On the beach at Freemans Bay, 1-, 2- or 3-bedroom comfortable, fully equipped and tasteful cottages and villas in different styles with an additional sofa bed and veranda. Spacious grounds, glorious views of the old dockyard at English Harbour and the many yachts at anchor, tennis, sunfish, windsurfing, beach bar and restaurant, ferry to Nelson's Dockyard.
$$$$ Nonsuch Bay Resort, Nonsuch Bay, T268-562 8000, www.nonsuch bayresort.net. Very spacious, comfortable and well-equipped apartments, villas and cottages on hillside with a popular sailing school suitable for all ages and abilities. The beach is man-made and there is sea grass on the seabed, but the infinity pool is lovely. Award-winning chef, food good but expensive. Close to **Harmony Hall** and Half Moon Bay for alternative eating out and beach.
$$$$ Siboney Beach Club, Dickenson Bay, T268-462 0806, www.siboneybeachclub.com. Proprietor Tony Johnson has made this one of the nicest small, independent places to stay. 12 comfortable suites in a 3-storey block on a private part of the beach. Decor and view vary but each has a bedroom, separate sitting/dining room with sofa bed, tiny kitchenette tucked away in a cupboard for making snacks, balcony, a/c, fan, CD player, phone. Pool, good restaurant,

The Coconut Grove, under separate management, watersports nearby.
$$$$ Tree Tops Cottage, Half Moon Bay, T268-460 4423, www.caribbeanavenue.com/treetops. Charming 2-bedroom, 2-bathroom West Indian-style villa with gingerbread fretwork on the veranda, perched on a hillside in open countryside 5 mins from Half Moon Beach. Daily maid service. Comfortable, breezy, with a lovely deck, where hummingbirds come to feed. Great place for relaxing and trying to spot dolphins and whales offshore, quiet, only the sounds of birds and goats, car needed.
$$$$ Villas at Sunset Lane, Sunset Lane, Paradise View, McKinnons, T268-562 7791, www.villasatsunsetlane.com. All-inclusive. On a hillside overlooking Dickenson Bay, this coral pink hotel is a very popular adults-only boutique establishment. Owned and run by chef Jackie who is outstandingly hospitable and produces delectable fusion cuisine. Pool, gym, pleasant gardens with fruit trees and veg which end up on your plate. Few mins' walk to the beach.
$$$$-$$$ Ocean Inn, English Harbour, T268-463 7950, www.theoceaninn.com. On a hillside overlooking English Harbour, with a spectacular and breezy view of the yachts and old buildings and a small pool. A rather haphazard appearance of rooms having been built below the main house when the owner felt like it. Rooms and bathrooms are small but adequate and but they have a TV, a/c, fridge, some of the cheaper rooms in the main house share a bathroom.

Breakfast is included, other meals on request, honour bar. Friendly owner and staff. 5-min walk down the hill to restaurants and bars.

$$$ Anchorage Rooms, 1421 Dockyard Drive, English Harbour, T268-561 0845, www.theanchorage rooms.com. Closed end Apr to end Sep. Decent accommodation just outside Nelson's Dockyard within easy reach of bars and restaurants so can be noisy. Rooms are simply furnished but comfortable with ceiling fans, mosquito nets, Wi-Fi and coolers provided for the beach. Very popular during Sailing Week and other sailing events. Dorm room available.

$$$ Ellen Bay Inn, Seatons, T268-561 6826, www.ellenbayinn.com. A small, family-run inn in the northeast, spacious rooms, simple but comfortable, good views from upstairs rooms, restaurant downstairs for all meals, flexible menu, very helpful staff. Free Wi-Fi, iPod dock, good a/c. Taxis, car and bicycle hire can be arranged, airport transfer US$20.

$$$ Wind Chimes Inn, Sir George Walter Highway, Carlisle, T268-728 2917, www.windchimesinn antigua.com. Right by the airport, convenient if you are island hopping or have a delayed flight. Aircraft noise during the day but no flights at night. Very helpful owners, comfortable rooms. Car hire nextdoor, 5 mins to Jabberwocky Beach.

$$$-$$ Paige Pond Country Inn, Buckley's Village, T268-562 5525, www.paigepondcountryinn.com. Inland, 2 green buildings overlooking Body Ponds, on a bus route. Rooms and suites, some linked for groups, good standard of furnishings, all with kitchenette, a/c, Wi-Fi, TV. Long-stay rates cheaper.

Barbuda *p39, map p39*
Several private homes offer accommodation, although these change if a long-term rental is taken. See www.barbudaful.net for further options.

$$$$ Barbuda Cottages, T268-720 3050, www.barbudacottages.com. Closed 1 Aug-1 Nov. On the southwest coast on a glorious stretch of beach next to **Uncle Roddy's Bar**. These 2 solar-powered rental properties (one with 3 bedrooms/2 bathrooms; another 1-bed cottage under construction in 2014) are in an idyllic position and very homely and comfortable with a veranda for sunset watching. Tours, activities and car hire can be arranged by owner, Kelcina Burton-George.

$$$$ Coco Point Lodge, in the far south, T268-462 3816, www.coco point.com. A hideaway since the 1960s and the ultimate in exclusivity, set on a stunning white-sand beach it occupies 164 acres of the peninsula at the tip of Barbuda, on probably the nicest beach in the whole Caribbean. There are rooms with shady verandas or cottages of different sizes with high ceilings, living room, bar and beach-front patio. With its own runway, guests are transferred from Antigua airport by a 12-min flight. Service is attentive and caring. Fishing and other watersports available on request, nothing is too much trouble.

$$$$ Lighthouse Bay Resort, T1-877-766 6718 toll-free, http://

lighthousebayresort.com. Sandwiched between a 17-mile pink-sand beach on the Caribbean and the lagoon, this small, all-suite hotel enjoys a tranquil and beautiful location, accessible only by helicopter or by boat. Comfortable with all modern amenities, watersports are offered, the food is good, service is excellent.

$$$$ North Beach, T268-721 3317, www.barbudanorthbeach.com. 5 simple cottages on stilts make up this isolated hideaway accessible only by boat. Owner Reuben James keeps it low key and rustic, but this no-frills approach isn't to everyone's taste when you've spent a lot of money getting there. Food is limited and there are no amenities. This is a place to escape modern life and do nothing except explore the beach and reef.

$$$ The Island Chalet, in the heart of Codrington, T268-460 0065, Mrs Pearline Askie. 4 rooms on the 1st floor with a small double bed and a rollaway, so they can sleep 3 at a pinch, but it gets a bit hot. Shared kitchen and living room facilities of a good standard, grocery across the square, bars and eating places a short walk away, price comes down at weekends when noise levels rise at night.

$$$ Palm Tree Guesthouse, T268-722 5496, palmtreegroup@live.com. Cerene Deazle runs this large and comfortable guesthouse about 15 mins' walk from Codrington, set in pretty gardens. All rooms have private bathroom and 2 connect to make a family suite. Meals available, Cerene has a bakery and restaurant in the village.

$$ Nedd's Guest House, Codrington, T268-778 5762, mcarthurnedd@hotmail.com. Run by Luke and Natalie Nedd, who can offer excursions and tours with fishing. They also run a supermarket downstairs and have a collection of 100 tortoises. 4 simple double rooms with shower room and balcony, shared sitting room and kitchen.

❼ Restaurants

Antigua *p29, maps p30, p32 and p35*

There are hundreds of restaurants and cafés on Antigua, some of which are very upmarket, some cater for the yachting fraternity and some for the local lunch crowd. There are several beach bars where you can spend the whole day relaxing and enjoying a leisurely lunch and a cold drink. Generally the standard of cooking is good, but service is often unhurried. VAT is 15%. 10% service is usually added to your bill. Prices are then comparable with the UK or USA.

$$$ Catherine's Café Plage, Pigeon Point Beach, English Harbour, T268-460 5050. Open 1200-2400. French chef, local ingredients, a great mix and one of the best restaurants on the island for lunch, dinner or drinks. Lovely setting right on the water overlooking the harbour, relaxed and beautiful.

$$$ Cecilia's High Point Café, Dutchman's Bay, T268-562 7070, http://highpointantigua.com. Mon, Thu 1200-2100, Fri-Sun 1200-1600, closed Tue, Wed. Traditional-style wooden house on the waterfront with tables on the veranda. There are swings for children and this is a great place to come for the day, spend time on the beach, shower off the sand and have a long, leisurely lunch or a romantic dinner. There are comfy chairs and sofas dotted around for relaxing and enjoying the view. Many people come here before catching their flight home as it is only 5 mins from the airport. Lovely food, very fresh fish and daily specials, menu written on a board always includes home made pasta and delicious desserts. Reservations essential.

$$$ Cloggy's Café, at the Yacht Club overlooking Falmouth Harbour, T268-460 6910, see Facebook. Daily in high season, closed Mon-Tue in summer. Popular with the sailing fraternity for its convenient location and hearty food, whether its burgers, brunch, tapas, seafood or steak. This is a 'see and be seen' place, lively and fun.

$$$ Coconut Grove, Siboney Beach Club, T268-462 1538, www.coconut groveantigua.com. Daily 0700-2300. On the beach, lovely spot with a typically Caribbean feel. Varied menu with seafood, steak, chicken and liberal use of coconut. Some local specialities but mostly international dishes. Good rum punches and non-alcoholic drinks too.

$$$ Harmony Hall, Brown's Bay, T268-460 4120, www.harmonyhall antigua.com. Daily 1200-1530, dinner 1930-2200 Wed-Sat, closed summer. Old plantation house and sugar mill dating back to 1843, now a restaurant and art gallery with accommodation, reached via several miles of unmetalled road or by boat to their dock. Bar is in an old mill, restaurant is on the patio overlooking Nonsuch Bay and Green Island. Lovely location, mostly Italian food, good but not cheap. **Harmony Hall Yacht Club** is here and races are organized. Pool, beach, complimentary boat trips to Green Island for guests.

$$$ HQ, upstairs in the historic Headquarters Building inside English Harbour, T268-562 2562. Daily, breakfast, lunch and dinner. Dining tables are inside and outside on the veranda overlooking Nelson's Dockyard, popular with a lively yachting crowd and there is live music some nights. Asian influences, plenty of fish; live lobster tank between diners and the open kitchen. Extensive wine and rum list. Dinner reservations suggested.

$$$ Jacqui O's Beach House, Crab Hill, Jolly Harbour, T268-562 2218, see Facebook. Tue-Sun 1000-2000, Mon lunch only. Excellent setting, on the beach, seating in the restaurant, at a high table by the bar or at picnic tables on the sand, Caribbean chic and very chilled. Excellent food, modern European fusion cuisine and very elegant, good wine and cocktail list. Luxurious beach sofas to relax on after your meal but they will cost you US$10.

$$$ Le Bistro, Hodges Bay, T268-462 3881, www.antigualebistro.com. Tue-Sun 1830-2230. Excellent French food prepared by head chef, Patrick Gauducheau. One of the best restaurants on the island and featured in international magazines and TV programmes. Varied menu includes vegetarian options and melt-in-the-mouth pastries, with an excellent wine list. Reservations required.

$$$ Papa Zouk, Hilda Davis Drive, Gambles, St John's, T268-464 6044, see Facebook. Mon-Sat from 1900 in season, otherwise Wed-Sat. Unprepossessing and casual place known for its specialities of bouillabaisse, a meal in itself, paella Créole, fresh fish and seafood, although chicken and meat is also available and vegetarian food on request. Congenial host, Bert Kirchner, goes through the daily specials with you and chats at the table while zouk music is played in the background. Huge selection of rums, Bert considers this a rum shop with food. Very popular, always full.

$$$ Sheer Rocks, Cocobay Resort, south of Jolly Harbour, T268-464 5283, www.sheer-rocks.com. Tapas lunch Wed-Mon from 1200, à la carte dinner Wed-Sat, Mon from 1800. Perched on rocks with a lovely sea view and waves splashing below you. Day beds and plunge pool enhance a leisurely lunch and the sunset-facing setting is very romantic for a special evening meal. Chef can accommodate special requirements, reservations essential.

$$$-$$ Café Napoleon, Redcliffe Quay, T268-562 1802, see Facebook. Open 0800-1600. In the heart of St John's close to the cruise ships, a great spot for casual breakfast and lunch, good food, drinks and snacks, popular with islanders and business people as well as visitors.

$$$-$ Quay Bar & Grill, Redcliffe St, St John's, T268-562 8147, thequayantigua@gmail.com. Daily 1000-2300. Formerly the Commissioner Grill, although it has been refurbished it remains a casual restaurant on the street corner in the heart of town, high ceilings and ceiling fans cool things down. West Indian dishes with plenty of seafood, lobster, steak, chicken, burgers, ribs and salads. Good rum punch. Popular with local people at lunchtime. About the only place in town open on Sun.

$$ Lion Pavilion, East Bus Sation, St John's, T268-771 4803, see Facebook. Open 0900-1700. Ital vegan food, lots of variety, menu changes daily depending on what is fresh and available, colourful, healthy and tasty. Great juices and desserts too.

$$-$ Australian, Redcliffe Quay, St John's. Mon-Sat 1000-2200, Sun 1500-2100. The best ice-cream bar on the island, rich and creamy, as well as chocolates, waffles, coffee and other delights. The machine making ice cream and sorbets takes centre stage in the room so you can see how it is made. Lots of flavours and cool bags offered if you want to take supplies away.

$$-$ Roti King, St Mary's St, St John's, T268-462 2328. Great place to come for a filling lunch with really good roti, popular with school children and office workers, everyone very friendly. Limited seating at lunch but you can get a takeaway. No prizes for appearance but that doesn't affect its popularity.

$$-$ Turner's Beach Bar, Valley Rd, Bolans, T268-462 9133. Daily 1000 until everyone goes home. Beach bar at the end of a long stretch of sand with a covered terrace or umbrellas on the beach. You can get breakfast, lunch, snacks, drinks or dinner. Local food, good selection, salads, huge roti, fish and chips, tender conch.

Barbuda *p39, map p39*

Always phone in advance to make a reservation as most places open only on demand and they will need to get enough food in for your visit. Transport can usually be arranged at the same time. If you are self-catering, do your shopping for fresh produce in the morning before it runs out. Many local specialities are seasonal, such as deer, conch, land crab and lobster, while availability of fish depends on whether the fishermen have been able to go out in their boats.

$$$-$$ ArtCafé, Two Foot Bay Rd, T268-460 0434, see Facebook. Owner and artist, Claire Frank, runs this café, gift shop and art gallery. Choose from a variety of teas or juices, coffee and cake. There is usually a dish of the day at lunchtime and dinner is on request. Friendly and informative hosts.

$$$-$$ Outback, Low Bay, T268-721 3280 (Jala) or T268-721 1972 (Calvin). Wonderful location on the 14-mile pink-sand beach between the sea and the lagoon. People come here for lunch on a day tour or you can arrange lunch or dinner any time, usually lobster, fish or chicken. Call for transport and reservations.

$$$-$$ Uncle Roddy's, Ocean Drive on the beach at Spanish Well Point, T268-785 3268. Advance bookings required to make sure that Roddy is there and cooking. Laid-back, island style, but delicious food including local lobster and barbecue chicken, served with rice, plantains and salad, washed down with a cold beer or other cold drinks. Roddy is full of stories and will pick you up if you wish.

$$ Lynton's, Codrington, T268-721 2796, lyntonthomas@ymail.com. Lynton Thomas has a bar and fast food place together with a shop under his **$$$ Bus Stop B&B**. You can get chicken and chips, burgers and hot dogs, drinks and ice cream, or he can arrange breakfast, lunch or dinner to order. Lynton also offers a taxi and tour service.

$$-$ AJ's, Codrington, T268-728 4334. Open 1500-2200, 2300 at weekends, reservations not needed. A popular fast food place serving burgers and pizza with soft drinks. Bring your own beer or other alcohol. Jordan and Kelcina show movies on an outdoor screen. Sit at picnic tables outside or on the veranda under cover.

🍸 Bars and clubs

Antigua *p29, maps p30, p32 and p35*

One of the live bands on the circuit is Spirited Band, a party band playing everything from soca, calypso, reggae, R&B and other popular styles. They include among their line-up rhythm guitarist Richie Richardson and bass guitarist Curtly Ambrose, better known to the world as famous West Indies cricketers. They also play during Sailing Week, cricket events and for private parties, although Richardson has cricket commitments and is not always available. See Facebook for when and where they are playing. The website www.antiguanice.com has daily listings of what's on.

Abracadabra, Dockyard Drive at the entrance to Nelson's Dockyard, English Harbour, T268-460 2701, http://theabracadabra.com. Bar 1800-late. Italian restaurant and video bar with a deck under the palm trees which is nearly always lively with dancing late into the night. Resident and visiting DJs and sometimes live bands. Particularly busy during Sailing Week. Casual, no strict dress code.

BeachLimerZ, Fort James Beach, T268-562 8574, www.beachlimerz.com. Open from 1100, happy hour Mon-Fri 1700-1900. Attractive wooden beach bar, popular with Antiguans as well as visitors. Good food, great cocktails and other drinks, nice sunbeds available for guests. Live music, comedy, reggae nights. Sat local soups when you can try goat water, bull foot soup or corn soup, Sun barbecue from 1300.

C&C Wine Bar, Redcliff Quay, T268-460 7025. Mon-Sat 1130-late. Next to the **Pottery Shop**, a wine bar and bistro in an historic building serving South African wines and a range of menu options, very popular with the local professional crowd and shoppers as well as tourists.

DBoat, Jolly Harbour, T268-734 2628, www.dboatantigua.com. Daily 1100-2400, happy hour 1700-1800, but on Sun from 1200 they have a DJ followed by a live band

at sunset. A party boat with a difference as this is a 1974 oil tanker moored offshore and you have to get a 10-min ferry out there, hourly from Crow's Nest, Jolly Harbour. There is a huge water slide, restaurant for lunch and dinner and a bar.

Mad Mongoose, Dockyard Drive, English Harbour, T268-463 7900. Daily from 1500. Restaurant and bar in a large wooden shack overlooking the harbour. Loud music attracts the younger yachting crowd. Live music Fri nights and every night during Sailing Week. Deck with outside seating.

Miller's by the Sea, on Fort James beach, T268-462 9414. Daily 0800-2200. Good beach bar with changing rooms and showers. Serves breakfast, lunch, dinner or just drinks, sometimes has live music but background music is usually reggae, owned by a local jazz hero. Fri night karaoke and barbecue 2000-2400 with half price drinks 1700-2100. Sun buffet brunch 1130-1630, US$11, with dancing on the sand.

Putters Bar and Grill, Dickenson Bay, T268-463 4653. Mon-Sat 1700-late, happy hour 1800-1900. Nightly specials vary from hot dogs to T-bone steaks, reasonable prices. Activities for families, crazy golf, Jungle Gym with swings, slides, climbing frames, ropes and ladders, air hockey, pinball and pool tables. Thu quiz night.

Shirley Heights Lookout, T268-460 1785, VHF 68, www.shirleyheights lookout.com. Daily lunch and dinner. Sun 'Jump Up' with steel band 1600-1900 followed by reggae 1900-2200. Very touristy but fun party, with barbecued burgers, chicken, ribs and salad at stalls on the hill overlooking English Harbour. Bus loads of revellers are brought from hotels all round the island and while the steel band is good family entertainment, it can get rowdy by the time the reggae band comes on if people have been drinking all afternoon.

Barbuda *p39, map p39*
Green Door, in the centre of Codrington, T268-460 0065. The island's first bar, run by Byron Askie, who can be found most days serving food and drinks from his snackette at the wharf by the lagoon where he cooks up traditional breakfasts at the weekend. Byron plays a mixture of music, from soul to soca.
Lyme, by the lagoon in Codrington. Used as a Mas Tent for Caribana, this bar and dance club doesn't keep regular hours, but is sometimes open Fri night, occasionally Sun and for special occasions.
Madison, Madison Sq, Codrington, T268-562 4073. Daily from 1800. A small bar with a wide range of drinks as well as occasional live music, karaoke and sports on TV.

⊕ Entertainment

Antigua *p29, maps p30, p32 and p35*
Deluxe Cinema, High St and Cross St, St John's, T268-462 3664, www.deluxecinemas.com and Facebook. A duplex showing all the latest releases. Tickets usually cost EC$10.

King's Casino, Heritage Quay, T268-462 1727, www.kingscasino.com. Table games, 350 slots (including Colossus, the world's largest slot machine), bingo, live entertainment on Fri, Sat nights.
Majestic Isle Casino - MIC, Dickenson Bay, T268-734 4777, http://themic.com. Daily 1900-0200. Opened end 2013, this new casino has 100 slot machines and 8 table games, sports bar, restaurant.

○ Shopping

Antigua *p29, maps p30, p32 and p35*
Art and crafts
For a directory of Antiguan artists, see http://antiguanartists.com.
Art at the Ridge, Sugar Ridge Village, near Jolly Harbour, T268-728 1558, see Facebook. Art gallery and shop opposite, with exhibitions of work by local artists Nov-Apr and wide variety of arts and crafts in the shop year-round.
Fig Tree Studio Art Gallery, Fig Tree Drive, T268-460 1234, www.figtreestudioart.com. Nov-Jun Mon-Sat 0930-1730. The studio and gallery of sculptor Sallie Harker (www.sallieharker.com) showcasing lots of local and regional art and crafts.
Harmony Hall, Brown's Bay Mill, near Freetown, T268-460 4120, www.harmonyhallantigua.com. Nov-Apr daily 1000-1800. An art gallery and gift shop, exhibiting and selling paintings, sculpture and crafts from leading Caribbean artists, popular for a lunch stop (see Restaurants, above) while touring by car or yacht.

Sarah Fuller's Pottery Shop, Redcliffe Quay, St John's, T268-462 5503, www.sarahfullerpottery.com. Mon-Fri 0930-1600. Lovely pottery and interesting designs by Sarah Fuller, hand crafted using local clay while some of the glazes use ash from Montserrat's volcano. You can visit the studio on the beach, 2 miles north of the airport, well signposted, where they will make anything to order. Her work is also exhibited at **Harmony Hall** and some hotel gift shops.

Markets

Market day in St John's is Sat but the main market is open Mon-Sat. The market building is at the south end of Market St opposite West St bus station, but there are goods on sale all around. In season, there is a good supply of fruit and vegetables. On Sat the market is busy from 0530 with stalls inside and outside the main building. There is also a small craft market attached to the market building.

Shopping centres

Heritage Quay and **Redcliffe Quay**, St John's. Shopping complexes with expensive duty-free shops (and public toilets) in the former. The latter has bars and restaurants and boutiques and a parking lot, free if you are shopping there. Some tourist shops offer 10% reductions to locals and compensate by overcharging tourists. Duty-free shops at the airport are more expensive than those in town.

Woods Mall, Friar's Hill Rd, is a modern shopping mall with a wide variety of shops including **The Epicurean Supermarket**, the most modern and best-stocked supermarket on the island, daily 0700-2300, a drugstore, post office and dental clinic.

Jolly Harbour is a good place for day-to-day shopping, and also has a large **Epicurean Supermarket**, open 0700-2100.

⏱ What to do

Antigua *p29, maps p30, p32 and p35*
The *Antigua Sports Calendar*, www.antiguasportscalendar.com, lists all the sporting events throughout the year in Antigua and Barbuda.

Cycling

Bike Plus, Independence Drive, St John's, T268-462 2453, see Facebook. Mon-Sat. Mountain bike rental, US$17.50 a day.
Paradise Boat Sales Rentals and Charters, T268-460 7125, www.paradiseboats.com. Daily. Rents mountain bikes as well as boats.
Salty Dogs Rentals, Jolly Harbour Commercial Centre, T268-783 5366, www.saltydogsrentals.com. Rents mountain bikes, scooters and colourful Jumby mokes.

Diving

Dive shops, many of which are based at hotels, are located all round the island.

Cricket

Cricket is the national sport and Antigua has produced many famous cricketers, including captains of the West Indies team Sir Viv Richards and Richie Richardson; fast bowlers Andy Roberts and Curtly Ambrose, Kenneth Benjamin, Eldine Baptiste and Winston Benjamin. In 2007 the brand new **Sir Vivian Richards Cricket Stadium** was inaugurated in time for the Cricket World Cup. Located between St John's and the airport on Factory Road, renamed the Sydney Walling Highway for the occasion, it was built with the help of the Chinese, who also paid for most of its construction. It has a permanent capacity of 10,000, but temporary stands boosted that to 20,000 for the World Cup. Although it is a multi-purpose stadium, it is used principally for cricket and has all the technology required of a world-class facility, with a practice pitch, training infrastructure and a media centre as well as underground tunnels for the players to use. Test matches can also be played at the **Antigua Recreation Ground** (ARG to locals) which remains the national stadium although the stand is rather dilapidated. Matches are helped along by lots of music and entertainment, carnival-style, and any break in play is filled by noise from the crowd. Brian Lara scored his world record 375 here in 1994 and again in 2004 with 400 not out, both times against England.

There is also a good cricket pitch at the **Jolly Beach Hotel** (where the teams usually stay), which is used as a practice ground during an international match, team training for the West Indies and for touring teams. The **Stanford Cricket Ground** by the airport has not been used since Allen Stanford was arrested in 2009 and later convicted for fraud and sentenced to 110 years in a US prison.

There are matches between Antiguan teams and against teams from other islands, and local matches can be seen in St John's near the market and all over the island in the evenings and at weekends. The **West Indies Cricket Board**, T268-460 5462, has information on Test Matches. The cricket season runs from January to July. For details of matches coming up, see www.cricschedule.com/venue/antigua.php.

Dive Antigua, next to the **Halcyon Beach Hotel**, T268-462 3483, http://diveantigua.com. The oldest dive operation on the island, 'Big John' (now retired from going under the boat) also gives a mini marine biology class and can give lots of advice on diving around Antigua.
Jolly Dive, on the beach in Jolly Harbour, T268-462 8305, www.jollydive.com. Office open Mon-Fri 0800-1200, 1300-1530, Sat 0730-1100,

Diving around Antigua

Diving is mostly shallow, up to 60 ft, except below **Shirley Heights**, where dives are up to 110 ft, or **Sunken Rock**, with a depth of 120 ft and where the cleft rock formation gives the impression of a cave dive. Popular sites are **Cades Reef**, which runs for 2½ miles along the leeward side of the island and is an underwater park; **Sandy Island Reef**, covered with several types of coral and only 30 ft to 50 ft deep; **Horseshoe Reef**, **Barracuda Alley** and **Little Bird Island**. There are also some wrecks to explore, including the *Andes*, in 20 ft of water in Deep Bay, but others have disappeared in hurricanes.

dive boats go out at 0900 and 1300. Near Cades Reef. Very experienced operation, takes safety very seriously but the staff are great fun too. There are always 2-3 Dive Masters in the water with you, another crew member stays on board the boat, they are all very helpful getting you in and out of the water, useful if the waves are choppy or there is a surge. 2-tank dive including all equipment US$124. Full range of PADI courses, Open Water qualification costs US$499.

Fishing

Nightwing, Falmouth Harbour, T268-464 4665, www.fishantigua.com. A 31-ft or 35-ft Bertrum, US$680 for 6 hrs, US$800 for 8 hrs, plus tip, maximum 6 people, split charters, good for beginners or experienced fishermen.
Overdraft, English Harbour, T268-720 4954, www.antiguafishing.com. A 40-ft fishing boat leaves from Nelson's Dockyard, US$495 for 4 hrs, US$650 for 6 hrs, or US$790 for 8 hrs.

Golf

Cedar Valley, near St John's, T268-462 0161, www.cedarvalleygolf.ag. An 18-hole, par-70 championship course which sometimes gets dried out but has pleasant coastal views. There is a driving range and pros are available. Green fees are US$49 for 18 holes. The Antigua Open is played here in Nov.
Jolly Harbour, T268-462 7771 ext 608, www.jollyharbourantigua.com/golf. A par-71 championship course in a parkland setting with 7 lakes, designed by Karl Litton. US$57.50 for 18 holes. Clubhouse, pro-shop, rental, tuition, restaurant.

Hiking

In the Nelson's Dockyard National Park there are 5 trails up to 1½ miles long in the hills, past fortifications and with fantastic views. Pick up a copy of *A Guide to the Hiking Trails in the National Park* at the museum or entrance to the dockyard. Hikes are arranged to historical and natural attractions and can be a good way of seeing the island. The **Historical and**

Archaeological Society organizes monthly hikes free of charge. **Hash House Harriers** arranges hikes/runs off the beaten track every other Sat at 1600, free of charge, contact Karen Whitehead, T268-464 8609, Karen@bluewaters.net. The **Environmental Awareness Group** offers monthly excursions, or field trips, T268-462 6236, www.eagantigua.org. Another hiking group is **5AM Hikers**, contact Oral Evenson, T268-727 0190, or Connie Richmond, T268-721 0145, for where to meet. Every Sat at 0500 they hike 3-4 miles, exploring the island. There can be up to 70 walkers as this is popular with Antiguans, free of charge although donations to a good cause sometimes requested. See Facebook group.

Footsteps Rainforest Hiking Tours, Fig Tree Drive, T268-460 1234, www.hikingantigua.com. Dassa Spencer leads walks starting from Fig Tree Studio Art Gallery to Wallings Dam, through the rainforest and up Signal Hill, Tue, Thu 0900, 2 hrs, US$45 adults, US$25 children under 16, moderate fitness required, water provided. Other walks can be custom designed, depending on what you want to do.

Sailing

For cruisers or bareboat charters Antigua offers good provisioning and marine supplies, with facilities to haul out boats at Antigua Slipway or Jolly Harbour. There are several marinas: **Nelson's Dockyard Marina** (www.nationalparksantigua.com); **Antigua Yacht Club Marina** (www.aycmarina.com); **Falmouth Harbour Marina** (www.antigua-marina.com); **Catmaran Marina** (www.catamaranmarina.com); and **Jolly Harbour Marina** (www.jolly-harbour-marina.com). Other sites worth visiting include the **Antigua & Barbuda Marine Association**, www.abma.org and www.antiguamarineguide.com.

Adventure Antigua, T268-726 6355, www.adventureantigua.com. Eco-tour by boat around the North Sound islands, exploring those less visited, snorkelling, lunch and drinks for US$115. Also complete tour of the island by speedboat, US$170, with stops at Stingray City, lunch on Green Island, Nelson's Dockyard, snorkelling at the Pillars of Hercules and relaxing at Rendezvous Bay, or a classic yacht tour on a 40-ft wooden Carriacou sloop, US$170, with snorkelling on Cades Reef and a lunch stop at Carlisle Bay. Book any tour online for 10% discount.

Antigua Yacht Club, English Harbour, T268-460 1799, www.antiguayachtclub.com. Holds races every Thu and those wishing to crew should listen to English Harbour Radio at 0900 on VHF 68/06 that morning. The sailing centre is open daily 0900-1800.

Jolly Harbour Yacht Club, Jolly Harbour Marina, just south of Ffryes Point, Antigua, T268-462 6042, http://jhycantigua.com. Holds Sat races as well as the **Red Stripe Regatta** in Feb and **Jolly Harbour Regatta** in Sep. There are 150 slips (103 fully serviced) for yachts of up to 260 ft and 12 ft draft, with a mega yacht facility.

Ondeck, T268-562 6696, www.ondeckoceanracing.com/antigua/montserrat-adventure.htm. On request, sailing trips are offered to Montserrat on a 60-ft Farr ocean racing yacht, leaving Falmouth Harbour at 0800, arriving Little Bay 1200. The return journey departs Montserrat at 1300, arriving 1800, US$189. Trips are flexible if you want to stay longer or overnight.

Wadadli Cats, T268-462 4792, www.wadadlicats.com. 3 routes offered: around the island (US$110); to Cades Reef (US$95); and to Bird Island (US$95). Guests are picked up from their hotels in the northwest before sailing down to Cades Reef for snorkelling, lunch, then a stop on Turners Beach before being dropped off again at their starting point. The trip to Bird Island also has snorkelling and swimming and the circumnavigation trip stops at Green Island for lunch.

Tennis

Many of the large hotels have courts; **Carlisle Bay Hotel** has a large tennis centre, see above, while **Curtain Bluff** offers tennis weeks coached by former international stars such as Tracy Austin, Fred Stolle, Tom Gullikson or Annabelle Croft.

Jolly Harbour Sports Centre, Jolly Harbour, T268-462 7771. 0800-2100. Lit tennis courts (US$20 per hr) and a kids' tennis academy.

Temo Sports, English Harbour, Antigua, T268-463 6376, VHF 68. Mon-Sat 0700-2200 in season, reduced hours in summer. A tennis/squash club open to the public with floodlit tennis courts, glass-backed squash courts, bar, bistro, equipment rental, round-robin tennis tournament every Fri 1730-2030, no credit cards.

Watersports

A wide range of watersports is available, with waterskiing, windsurfing, parasailing, snorkelling, kayaking, kitesurfing and swimming with stingrays. Dickenson Bay is the only beach with public hire of watersports equipment, but some hotels will hire to the public, especially out of season. The **Sandals Grande** all-inclusive resort on Dickenson Bay allows adult day visitors (US$110.50 per person 1000-1800 or 1800-0200; US$188 1000-0200), including use of all sports facilities, meals, bar, etc. **Jolly Beach Resort & Spa** offers a single day pass of US$75 per adult, US$45 for children, 0900-1700, plus US$50 if you want the use of a room for the day. Most watersports operators offer hotel transfers.

Antigua Paddles, T268-720 4322, www.antiguapaddles.com. Offers an excellent half-day eco-tour of the mangroves and islands off the northeast shore with kayaking, snorkelling and hiking.

Kitesurf Antigua, Jabberwock Beach, T268-720 5483, T268-460 3414 after 1800, www.kitesurfantigua.com. Open 0900-1700. IKO-approved school offering kitesurfing lessons, rentals and sales.

Sting Ray City, Seatons, T268-562 7297, www.stingraycityantigua.com. Snorkellers can interact with stingrays, wading or swimming with them and feeding them. The rays are confined in a spacious pen on a sand bank in the sea.

Windsurf Antigua, Dutchman's Bay north of the airport, T268-461 9463, www.windsurfantigua.net. Instruction to beginners (guarantee to achieve in 2 hrs or no charge), intermediate and advanced windsurfers. Patrick Scales has a mobile operation and will travel to any hotel.

Barbuda *p39, map p39*
Cycling
Barbuda Bike Tours/Cycle Rental, Ginnery St, Codrington, T268-773 9599, see Facebook. Bicycle and kayak rental. Owner Jonathon Pereira is on the island 4 months of the year.

Horse riding
Horses can be hired in Codrington.

Tour operators
Day tours include the Bird Sanctuary, Highland House, the caves and the Martello tower, anything can be arranged, eg bicycles, horse riding, hiking. The **Barbuda Taxi Association** will do tours, T268-727 9957. Before booking a boat tour, check whether the boat has lifejackets, communication equipment and insurance in the event of an accident. The **Barbuda Express** ferry (see Transport in the Leeward Islands, page 10), offers a tour of the frigate bird colony, lunch and a cruise along the coast with stops for swimming and snorkelling.

Barbuda Outback Tours, T268-721 3280 (Jala) or T268-721 1972 (Calvin). Land or boat tours, taking in the frigate birds, the Martello tower, the caves, fishing, birdwatching and lunch on the beach.

John Taxi Service and Tours, T268-723 5012, see Facebook. Island tours with Levi John, a knowledgeable guide who tops off any tour by offering a barbecue lunch on the pink-sand beach at his own beach bar, **River Beach Bar & Grill**, where you can have freshly grilled lobster, fish, chicken or conch.

⊖ Transport

Antigua *p29, maps p30, p32 and p35*
Air
V C Bird Airport, some 4½ miles from St John's, is the centre for air traffic in the area with flights from the UK, USA and the Caribbean. See page 6 for details.

Caribbean Helicopters, T268-460 5900, www.caribbeanhelicopters.com. Head office and hangar at the airport and a helipad for cruise ship visitors at Fort Rd, St John's. Daily custom charters and day trips; half-island tour, 20 mins, US$145 per person; full-island tour, 30 mins, US$185; Montserrat Volcano tour, 50 mins, US$285.

Boat
See page 10 for details of the **Barbuda Express** ferry between Antigua and Barbuda. Take your passport.

Bus

Buses are banned from north of the line from the airport to St John's, but run frequently between **St John's** and **English Harbour**, US$1.40. There are also buses from the east terminal by the war memorial to **Willikies**, from where it's a 20-min walk to **Long Bay Beach** and **Parham**. There are no buses to the airport and very few to beaches though 2 good swimming beaches on the way to Old Rd can be reached by bus. Bus frequency can be variable, and there are very few after dark or on Sun. Buses usually go when they are full, ask the driver where he is going. They are numbered and destinations are on display boards at the West Bus Station. Buses to **Old Road** are half hourly on average, though more frequent around 0800 and 1600. See www.bustopanu.com to calculate routes and fares.

Car hire

A local driving licence, EC$50, valid for 3 months, must be purchased on presentation of a foreign (not international) licence. There is a 24-hr petrol station on Old Parham Rd outside St John's. Petrol costs US$0.95 per litre everywhere.

A list of hire companies is available on the Board of Tourism website, www.antigua-barbuda.org, and on www.antiguanice.com. Rates are from US$45 per day, US$300 a week (no mileage charge), including insurance charges.

Taxi

Taxis have TX registration plates. In St John's there is a taxi rank on St Mary St, or outside the supermarket. They are not metered and frequently try to overcharge, or else have no change, so agree a price first, they should have a EC$ price list so ask to see it. There is a list of government-approved taxi rates posted in EC$ and US$ at the airport just after customs. If going to the airport early in the morning, book a taxi the night before as there are not many around. A day tour normally costs about US$72-120 for 1-4 people, or an hourly rate of US$24 for up to 4 passengers. Taxi excursions advertised in the hotels are generally overpriced. Tips for taxi drivers are usually 10%.

Barbuda *p39, map p39*
Air

There are 2 airports; the main one is just south of Codrington. Flights take 10 mins from St John's. The 2nd airport only serves Coco Point. There are no international flights and all immigration formalities are carried out on Antigua.

Boat

The **Barbuda Express** (www.barbuda express.com) catamaran ferry service runs 5 days a week depending on weather conditions. Expect the crossing to take 2 hrs, despite the advertised time. The boat is neither new nor particularly comfortable; it is a workhorse to get Barbudans and lobsters over to Antigua and supplies back again.

Car hire

There are not many cars available as spare parts are difficult to get hold of on the island and sometimes fuel runs out. It is possible to hire jeeps from **Shorelines Rentals**, T268-770 0166, shorelines@gmail.com. Small jeeps cost US$65 a day including insurance. A taxi tour (see above) may be more productive as your driver will also be an informative guide.

ⓘ Directory

Antigua *p29, maps p30, p32 and p35*

Medical services Mount St John's Medical Centre, is the new and main facility on the island, having replaced the old Holberton Public Hospital. It has a good A&E department and intensive care unit although most foreigners suffering serious accidents are airlifted out. **Adelin Medical Centre** is a private practice, T268-462 0866. Pharmacies are mostly in and around St John's; there are none in the English Harbour area. They are usually open Mon-Sat 0900-1700, although **Ceco Pharmacy**, High St, is open daily 0815-2400.

Barbuda *p39, map p39*

Immigration For those arriving by boat, **Customs**, T268-460 0085, **Immigration**, T268-764 2161/562 5551, Mon-Thu 0800-1630, Fri 0800-1500, Sat-Sun 1000-1400. **Medical services** Hannah Thomas Hospital, staffed by a Cuban doctor and Barbudan medical workers completing their training after studying in Cuba, together with qualified nursing staff. If you have a major medical emergency you will be airlifted off the island.

Top rum cocktails

There are hundreds of different rums in the Caribbean, each island claiming theirs is the best. The main producers are Jamaica, Cuba, Barbados, Guyana, Martinique and the Dominican Republic, but other islands such as St Kitts also produce excellent brands. Generally, the younger, light rums are used in cocktails while aged, dark rums are drunk on the rocks or treated as you might a single malt whisky.

Cocktails first became popular after the development of ice-making in the USA in 1870, but boomed in the 1920s partly because of prohibition in the USA and the influx of visitors to Cuba, the Bahamas and other islands, escaping stringent regulations. People have been drowning their rum in cola ever since the Americans brought bottled drinks into Cuba during the war against Spain at the end of the 19th century, hence the name, **Cuba Libre**.

One of the nicest and most refreshing cocktails is a **Daiquirí**, invented in Santiago de Cuba in 1898 by an engineer in the Daiquirí mines. The natural version combines 1½ tablespoons of sugar, the juice of half a lime, some drops of maraschino liqueur, 1½ oz light dry rum and a lot of shaved ice, all mixed in a blender and then served piled high in a wide, chilled champagne glass with a straw. You can also have fruit versions, with strawberry, banana, peach or pineapple, using fruit or fruit liqueur.

Another Cuban favourite is the **Mojito**, once popular with Ernest Hemingway and his friends in Havana and now very trendy in bars and clubs in Europe. Put half a tablespoon of sugar, the juice of half a lime and some lightly crushed mint leaves in a tall glass. Stir and mix well, then add some soda water, ice cubes, 1½ oz light dry rum and top up with soda water to taste. Garnish with mint leaves and serve with a straw.

Everybody has heard of the **Piña Colada**, which can be found on all the islands and is probably the most popular of the fruit-based cocktails, ideal by the side of the pool. Combine and blend coconut liqueur, pineapple juice, light dry rum and shaved ice, then serve with a straw in a glass, a pineapple or a coconut.

Many Caribbean hotels offer you a welcome cocktail on arrival. This is often an over-sweet, watered-down punch, with a poor quality rum and sickly fruit juice. The standard recipe for a **rum punch** is: 'one of sour, two of sweet, three of strong and four of weak'. If you measure that in fluid ounces, it comes out as 1 oz of lime juice, 2 oz of syrup (equal amounts of sugar and water, boiled for a few minutes), 3 oz of rum and 4 oz of water, fruit juices or ginger ale. You could add ice and a dash of Angostura Bitters from Trinidad, use nutmeg syrup from Grenada or Falernum from Barbados instead of sugar syrup, and garnish it with a slice of lime. Delicious.

Contents

Footprint features

Montserrat

Montserrat is like nowhere else. The Irish-influenced 'Emerald Isle' is totally unspoiled by tourism but its volcano has put it on the map, having wiped out the southern part of the island. Montserrat is mountainous, with three ranges of hills: Silver Hills, Centre Hills, and Soufrière Hills, and it is the 3000-ft Chances Peak in the Soufrière Hills that has been erupting since 1995. The south of the island, which like the rest of the island used to be all lush green, is now grey with ash and the former capital, Plymouth, is a modern Pompeii. The north was protected by the Centre Hills range, running east to west through the middle of the island and creating a 'safe' zone. Of the former population of 11,000, less than half remained a few years later, with many heading for new lives on Antigua or in the UK. Those remaining were relocated to the north, 'safe' zone, where they rebuilt their lives. The population is now increasing again, as business picks up and islanders return. Montserrat was off-limits to tourism for a few years, but the still-active volcano now attracts visitors. Here you can enjoy views of a glowing volcano, volcanic moonscapes, deserted black-sand beaches, a network of challenging mountain trails, historic sites, waters teeming with fish, coral and sponges, and some of the friendliest people in the region. Only the northern third of the island is populated because of the volcano and the inhabitants are developing the area in style.

Volcanic violence

In 1995 the lives of Montserratians were turned upside down when the 'dormant' volcano erupted. The residents of Plymouth and villages in the south were evacuated to the north as lava, rocks and ash belched from the Soufrière Hills for the first time since the 1930s. Activity increased in 1997; during March and April pyroclastic flows reached two miles down the south side of the volcano. The former tourist attractions of the Great Alps Waterfall and Galways Soufrière were covered, there was a partial collapse of Galways Wall and lava flowed down the Tar River Valley. In May the volcanic dome was growing at 3.7 cubic metres per second, and in June a huge explosion occurred when a sudden pyroclastic flow of hot rock, gas and ash poured down the volcano at 200 mph. It engulfed 19 people, destroyed seven villages and some 200 homes. The flow, which resulted from a partial collapse of the lava dome, came to within 50 yards of the sea, close to the airport runway, which had to be closed. The eruption sent an ash cloud six miles into the air and people were forced to wear ash masks. In August another bout of activity destroyed Plymouth, which caught fire under a shower of red hot lava. It now looks like a lunar landscape, completely covered by grey ash. In December 1997 there was a huge dome collapse which created a 600-yard amphitheatre around Galways Soufrière and destroyed several deserted communities. The White River delta was increased to about one mile and the water level rose by about 3 ft. During 1998-1999 dome collapses continued, with ash clouds at times up to eight miles high, but scientists reported that the dome, while still hot, was gradually cooling and entering a quieter phase. In 2000 there was further activity and in July 2003 the dome of the volcano collapsed again and a thick cloud of ash and rocks spread across the island. Since then activity has been relatively quiet although the volcano is still active.

Arriving in Montserrat

Getting there

John A Osborne Airport, in the north of the island at Gerald's, opened in 2005 to replace the one on the east coast which was buried by volcanic activity. **Fly Montserrat** and **SVG/ABM Air** provide several daily flights from Antigua with connecting flights from other islands. However, most people arrive by ferry from Antigua five days a week, or the weekly service from St Kitts and Nevis.

Montserrat

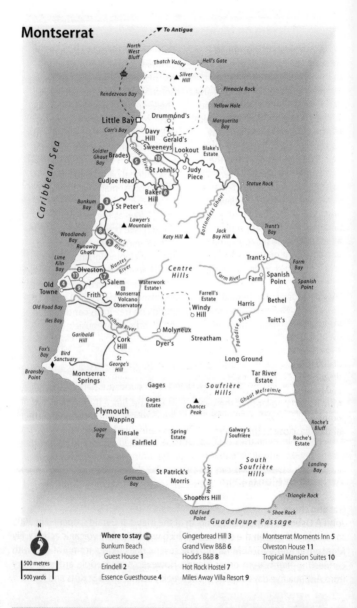

To Antigua

North West Bluff

Thatch Valley · Hell's Gate

Silver Hill ▲

Rendezvous Bay · Pinnacle Rock

Yellow Hole

Drummond's · Marguerita Bay

Carr's Bay

Little Bay □

Davy Hill · Gerald's ✈

Sweeneys · Lookout · Blake's Estate

Soldier Ghaut Bay · Brades · **5** · **10** · St John's · Judy Piece

Cudjoe Head · Baker Hill **6**

Statue Rock

Bunkum Bay **1** · St Peter's

Lawyer's Mountain ▲

Woodlands Bay · **8** · Lawyer's River · Katy Hill ▲ · Jack Boy Hill ▲

Runaway Ghaut · **2** · Trant's Bay

Lime Kiln Bay · Olveston · Nantes River

Old Towne · **11** · **4** · **7** · Salem · Centre Hills · Trant's · Farm Bay

9 · Frith · Waterwork Estate · Farrell's Estate · Farm · Spanish Point · Spanish Point

Monserrat Volcano Observatory · Windy Hill · Harris · Bethel · Tuitt's

Old Road Bay · Iles Bay

Bethan River · Molyneux · Dyer's · Streatham · Long Ground

Garibaldi Hill · Cork Hill

Fox's Bay · Bird Sanctuary · St George's Hill

Bransby Point · Montserrat Springs · Gages · Soufrière Hills · Tar River Estate

Gages Estate · Chances Peak ▲ · Ghaut Mefraimie

Plymouth · Wapping

Sugar Bay · Kinsale · Fairfield · Spring Estate · Galway's Soufrière · Roche's Bluff · Roche's Estate

Germans Bay · St Patrick's · Morris · White River · South Soufrière Hills · Landing Bay

Shooters Hill · Triangle Rock · Shoe Rock

Old Ford Point · *Guadeloupe Passage*

Caribbean Sea

N

500 metres
500 yards

Where to stay 🏠
Bunkum Beach Guest House **1**
Erindell **2**
Essence Guesthouse **4**

Gingerbread Hill **3**
Grand View B&B **6**
Hodd's B&B **8**
Hot Rock Hostel **7**
Miles Away Villa Resort **9**

Montserrat Moments Inn **5**
Olveston House **11**
Tropical Mansion Suites **10**

Fauna and flora on Montserrat

Natural vegetation is confined mostly to the summits of hills, where elfin woodlands occur. At lower levels, fern groves are plentiful and lower still are cacti, sage bush and acacias. Flowers and fruit are typical of the Caribbean with many bay trees, from which bay oil (or rum) is distilled, the national tree, the mango and the national flower, *Heliconia caribaea* (a wild banana known locally as 'lobster claw'). There are 34 species of bird resident on the island and many more migrants. Unique to Montserrat is the Montserrat oriole, *Icterus oberi*, a black and gold oriole named the national bird. There are also the rare forest thrush, the bridled quail dove, mangrove cuckoo, trembler and purple-throated carib. Many of these can be seen along the Centre Hills trail in the middle of the island between the ash-covered Soufrière Hills and the Silver Hills. The vegetation here is biologically diverse and supports a variety of wildlife. The Centre Hills area is the subject of a major environmental project which will see it developed as a national park. Montserrat cannot boast many wild animals, although it shares the terrestrial frog, known as the mountain chicken (see box, page 68), only with Dominica. Agoutis, bats and lizards, including iguanas which can grow to over 4 ft in length (they used to take the balls on the golf course, mistaking them for eggs), can all be found and tree frogs contribute to the island's 'night-music'.

Getting around

Driving is on the left. Roads are paved and fairly good, but narrow and twisty. There are many pebbles on the roads and you must be careful, especially on inclines. Drivers travel fast, passing on blind corners, with much use of their horns. There are several car hire companies. Hitching is safe and easy. The standard fare in minibuses is EC$3. Outside the fixed times and routes they operate as taxis and private journeys can be arranged with drivers. Taxis are usually small buses, which can be shared. Taxis and minibuses have green licence plates beginning with 'H'. Fares are set and listed by the Tourist Board.

Exclusion zone

The southern two thirds of the island are now off-limits and subject to an exclusion order following the eruption of the volcano and the evacuation and relocation of the population. It is illegal to enter as it is dangerous. The boundary runs from the coast north of Plymouth in a northeasterly direction between the Centre Hills and Soufrière Hills to the east coast just north of the old airport.

The Emerald Isle and its Irish-African heritage

Montserrat was settled by the British Thomas Warner, who brought English and Irish Catholics from their uneasy base in the Protestant island of St Kitts. Once established as an Irish-Catholic colony – the only one in the Caribbean – Catholic refugees fled there from persecution in Virginia and, following his victory at Drogheda in 1649, Cromwell sent some of his Irish political prisoners to Montserrat. By 1648 there were 1000 Irish families on the island. An Irishman brought some of the first slaves in 1651 and the economy became based on sugar. Slaves quickly outnumbered the original British indentured servants and today the vast majority of the people are of African descent. A slave rebellion in 1768, appropriately enough on St Patrick's Day, led to all the rebels being executed and today they are celebrated as freedom fighters.

The Irish influence can still be seen in national emblems. On arrival your passport is stamped with a green shamrock; while the island's flag and crest show a woman, Erin of Irish legend, complete with her harp. There are many Irish names, of both people and places, and the national dish, goat water stew, is supposedly based on a traditional Irish recipe. A popular local folk dance, the Bam-chick-a-lay resembles Irish step dances and musical bands may include a fife and a drum similar to the Irish bodhran. The new Government House at Woodlands has a shamrock fixed to its roof.

Places in Montserrat → *For listings, see pages 70-78.*

Little Bay
Plymouth, the former capital, is now covered by mud flows and only the tops of a very few buildings can be seen above the mud and ash. Administrative offices have moved to the Government Headquarters at **Brades** in the north of the island and Little Bay is being developed as a future capital. The port is here, as well as a public market and a sports/cricket ground. There are plans to build a marina for visiting yachts, many of which come over from Antigua, particularly after Sailing Week there.

A state-of-the-art cultural performance/convention centre, **Montserrat Cultural Centre** ⓘ *T664-4914242, www.themontserratculturalcentre.com*, was built in 2007, the brainchild of the former Beatles' producer, Sir George Martin, who was instrumental in fundraising for its construction. One of the most publicized events was the Music for Montserrat concert at the Royal Albert Hall in London in 1997. In 2009, Sir George and Sir Trevor Mcdonald helped to install a 'Wall of Fame' in the centre, made up of the handprints cast in bronze of the famous musicians who recorded at **Sir George's Air Studios** on Montserrat in the 1980s, including Sir Paul McCartney and Sir Elton John. The cultural centre has an auditorium seating 500, a conference centre, recording studio and gift shop, and is the venue for local concerts, festival, films and even banquets and weddings. There is also outdoor staging for open-air performances.

The north

The island's only white coral beach is at **Rendezvous Bay** to the north of Little Bay. There is no road access and it is a stiff one-hour hike along a steep, mountainous, 1.3-mile trail, which starts behind the concrete block company in Little Bay and climbs over a saddle before descending into Rendezvous valley and the beach. Take food, water and a hat; it is very hot and there is no shade on the beach. Avoid the poisonous manchineel trees and look out for the spiny sea urchins among the rocks at the north end. It is, however, a delightful and beautiful spot, unblemished by human interference. Snorkelling is good on the reef offshore, which is quite shallow and calm. The coral is healthy and abundant and you can often see stingrays and turtles as well as lots of reef fish. Fruit bats roost in Bat Cave, which you can swim in to. You can also take a boat to Rendezvous Bay, or walk there and arrange for a boat to come and pick you up.

There is another, longer hiking route to Rendezvous Bay which starts at Drummonds, north of the airport. At the end of the paved road, follow the dirt road north until you get to a junction of three tracks. Turn left, northwest through dry forest and open grassland until it drops down to Rendezvous Bay. Take a swim to cool off before heading over the saddle back to Little Bay. Drummonds is also the starting point to hike up Silver Hill (1322 ft), at the top of which is a communications mast and a great view to Antigua.

The west coast

Looking out to sea from Carr's Bay, south of Little Bay, you can see Redonda and, beyond that, Nevis. There is a small, ruined fort here with canon pointing out to deter invaders. There is also a replica of the War Memorial and Clock Tower that were destroyed in Plymouth. The rocks here are home to an iguana, which you can sometimes see sunbathing. The road south goes inland through Brades and Cudjoe Head, meeting the coast again at tiny Bunkum Bay. There are volcanic black-sand beaches here, which in reality means the sand may be a silvery grey or dark golden brown colour, and a bit further south at Woodlands Bay, where there are picnic tables and toilets.

On the main road in the Oriole Complex, Olveston, is the **Montserrat National Trust** ⓘ *T664-491 3086, www.montserratnationaltrust.ms, Mon-Fri 0830-1630, Sat on request 1000-1300*, which has exhibitions of Montserrat's culture and heritage as well as the natural environment. The exhibition for **St Patrick's Week** is usually a highlight and the mid-year **Calabash Festival**

Mountain chicken

'Mountain chicken' used to be a common sight in Montserrat, where it was known to steal the golf balls on the golf course and hide them in its burrows. In reality it is not chicken, but a frog, *Leptodactylus fallax*, that tastes a bit like chicken. One of the largest frogs in the world, it is currently found only in Dominica and Montserrat, although at one time it may have lived on at least seven islands. However, it is critically endangered, not just from over-hunting, introduced predators and habitat loss (the volcanic eruption on Montserrat devastated much of its habitat), but because of a pathogenic chytrid fungal skin condition, *Batrachochytrium dendrobatidis*, which has caused the population to plummet. Conservationists are working hard to save the species. Seven unaffected frogs were taken to ZSL London Zoo, where they are part of a captive breeding programme. The female lays her eggs in a foam-filled burrow and when the tadpoles hatch, she feeds them with infertile eggs which she lays every few days especially for the purpose. It is hoped that frogs bred at the zoo in a bio-secure, temperature-controlled environment will be released into the wild when the danger of fungal disease has receded. So far, trial releases have been carried out with frogs radio-tracked and monitored by teams of field researchers. It is hoped that by monitoring disease distribution and prevalence and testing samples, researchers may discover how the mountain frog can survive, making it a case study which could be applied to the global amphibian crisis. For more information see www.mountainchicken.org.

of arts and crafts is also interesting. As well as the exhibition hall, there is a research library with videos and photographs of Montserrat's history, gift shop (arts and crafts, maps and photographs) and a botanic garden. Tours are offered to show visitors the traditional medicinal herbs grown there as well as plants that have contributed to the island's economy and plants endemic to Centre Hills.

About half a mile from the National Trust is **Runaway Ghaut**, one of the many deep ravines that carry rainwater from the mountains to the sea. There is a saying that 'if you drink the waters from this burn, to Montserrat you will return.' Runaway Ghaut got its name because it was the escape route for the French when they were driven off the island in 1712 and the ravine on the other side of the road is called Frenchman's Creek.

The Belham Valley bridge, which connected the north to the south and the golf course, is now buried under volcanic debris. You can walk in the valley, but only when the weather is dry. An interesting beach to visit is the one at **Old Road Bay**, below the old Vue Pointe Hotel, which has been impacted by volcanic mudflows, creating strange patterns. The beach is now much bigger than it was and the original pier is now firmly on dry land. Be careful in rainy weather as mud can flow very quickly down the valley behind the beach. **Fox's Bay** is a deserted beach in a zone which at the height of the volcanic crisis was a no-go area and is now part of the Day Time Entry Zone. The beach is a delight. From the northern end of **Barton Bay**, below the abandoned Montserrat Springs Hotel in Richmond Hill, you can walk round to Fox's Bay at low tide. Take the road down to the old hotel beach bar.

Soufrière Hills Volcano
The Soufrière Hills volcano is now a tourist attraction and can best be viewed from the **Montserrat Volcano Observatory** ⓘ *T664-491 5647, www.mvo.ms, Mon-Thu 1015-1515, observation platform always open, US$4, US$2 children*, in Flemmings, where there is an Interpretation Centre. If the volcano is dangerously active visitors are excluded. Video shows of volcanic activity and a tour of the monitoring rooms and equipment are available, with volcanic artefacts and displays explaining the techniques used in monitoring seismic activity. From the observation platform you can see Plymouth and the abandoned Air Studios, destroyed by Hurricane Hugo in 1989. Spectacular views of the volcano and its damage can also be viewed in safety from the **Jack Boy Hill** picnic spot in the east, overlooking the old airport and villages now covered by pyroclastic flows, close to the start of the Exclusion Zone. From here you can see the grey, ash-covered flanks of what was Chances Peak, in stark contrast with the Centre Hills, which are still green, forested and fertile. This viewing spot is popular at night time as you get excellent views of the glowing dome. There is a viewing platform with telescope, barbecue pit, toilets and a short trail.

Centre Hills
The loss of two thirds of the island after the volcanic eruptions has left the Centre Hills as the last viable habitat for many of Montserrat's endemic and threatened wildlife. These include the mountain chicken (see box, opposite), the Montserrat oriole and the galliwasp lizard, as well as several species of plants. The **Centre Hills Project** ⓘ *T664-491 2075, www.malhe.gov.ms/centrehills*, is part of an ongoing scientific study to enable sustainable use and management of the forest resources, the hills being the source of all the island's water supply. The public is being involved in education, fieldwork and consultation. Funded by the Darwin Initiative for the Survival of Species, the project is being led by the Royal Society for the Protection of Birds (RSPB) in partnership with the Montserrat Tourist Board, Montserrat National Trust, Ministry of Agriculture, Lands, Housing and Environment, the Durrell Wildlife Conservation Trust and

the Royal Botanic Gardens (Kew, London). Anyone interested in finding out more about the area's ecology and hiking trails should buy *The Guide to Centre Hills*, EC$40/US$14, which has lots of detailed information and can be bought from the Montserrat Tourist Board or the Montserrat National Trust. The **Oriole Trail** is a very popular walk of 1.3 miles which, with a guide, takes about two hours as you stop to look and listen for birds, principally the oriole, or examine plants. The trail climbs up Lawyers Mountain and a clearing at the top affords fabulous views of the island to both the north and south.

◉ Montserrat listings

For hotel and restaurant price codes and other relevant information, see pages 12-16.

◯ Where to stay

Montserrat *p61, map p64*
Hotel tax is 10%; guesthouses, B&Bs and villas are subject to a 7% tax. There is only 1 hotel but many villas and apartments to rent, see www.visitmontserrat.com.

$$$$-$$$ Miles Away Villa Resort, Mayfield Estate Drive, Olveston, T664-491 7362, www.milesawayvillaresort.com. Standard rooms, suites with kitchenettes or 3-bedroom villa, on hillside with good views and a short trail down to a river, lovely grounds and large pool. The helpful owners can arrange anything for you.

$$$$-$$$ Tropical Mansion Suites, Sweeneys, T664-491 8767, www.tropicalmansion.com. 2-storey 16-room hotel in the north of the island, views over Little Bay and the sunset from some rooms, small pool, family-run. Bar and restaurant with good food. Friendly staff and service. Popular with holiday-makers as well as government and business visitors.

$$$ Erindell, Gros Michel Drive, Woodlands, T664-491 3655, www.erindellvilla.com. 2 pleasant rooms alongside the family home, twin beds can be made up as king, private bathroom, TV, Wi-Fi, fans, fridge, microwave oven and toaster. 3 meals available, dinner eaten with hosts. Welcome pack of snacks, fruit and drinks. Pool outside the rooms, free laundry, complimentary snorkelling equipment, beach towels, beach mats and umbrellas, no credit cards. 1-min walk to a bus route, 15-min walk to Woodlands Beach.

$$$ Hodd's B&B, Woodlands, T664-491 5248, www.visitmontserrat.net/forest-guestsuite. David and Maureen Hodd offer the **Rainforest Guest Suite** attached to their home. A good breakfast is included and there is a microwave and fridge for preparing snacks. Outside there is a small pool with waterfall and a barbecue. Other meals available on request.

$$$ Olveston House, Olveston, T664-491 5210, www.olvestonhouse.com. This iconic guesthouse is the family home of George Martin, the producer and owner of **Air Studios** since the early 1980s, previous guests include famous recording artists such as Paul McCartney, Sting, Elton John and Eric Clapton. Closed for 1 month each year for family use, it is now a charming place to stay in 5 acres of lovely grounds, with 6 spacious rooms, Wi-Fi, excellent restaurant, bar with delicious cocktails, pool and tennis.

$$$-$$ Bunkum Beach Guest House (Palm Loop Cottage), Bunkum Bay, T664-491 2124, http://palmloopcottage.com. Sun and Kristina Lea run this comfortable house overlooking Woodlands Beach and a short walk from Bunkum Beach. Good snorkelling and hiking on Centre Hills trails within 10-min walk and buses practically on the doorstep. Poolside suite with kitchenette or 2-bedroom villa, or rent the whole complex for privacy. Pool, lovely sunsets, tame iguanas on the rocks. Sunny does a wonderful tour of the island and Kristina is extremely helpful.

$$$-$$ Essence Guesthouse, Old Towne, T664-491 5411, www.essencemontserrat.com. On a hillside with views of the volcano, Belham Valley and the beach. Self-catering 1-bedroom apartment and 1 guest room, each with its own entrance and patio. Car hire and excursions can be arranged. Eric and Annie from Belgium are very friendly hosts.

$$$-$$ Gingerbread Hill, St Peter's, T664-491 5812, www.volcano-island.com. David and Clover Lea run a delightful guesthouse with incredible views and lovely 3-acre garden. Several options for accommodation: rooms in a separate house, including

a backpacker's special in a basic room, or you can rent the whole house, or take the charming suite adjoining their own house, bathroom, deck, fridge, TV, meals on request. Camping equipment is available, also bikes and a rental car. Family atmosphere, very friendly and hospitable. They also run **Hill Top Café** and their son has the **Bunkum Beach Guest House** if you want a 2-centre stay.

$$$-$$ Grand View B&B, Baker Hill, T664-491 2284, www.mnigrandview.com. 6 rooms and 2 suites, 2 of the rooms share a bathroom and are cheaper, Wi-Fi, lunch and dinner with reservation. Not the most atmospheric place to stay, but the view is grand, and the owner is knowledgeable and helpful. Food is local and tasty with herbs from the garden and the bar is lively, with darts and pool.

$$$-$$ Montserrat Moments Inn, Manjack Heights, T644-491 7707, flogriff@candw.ms. A family home renting rooms with TV, fridge, a/c or fan, shared or private bathroom. Breakfast is included, other meals by reservation, or you can use the shared kitchenette. Email and laundry available. Credit cards accepted. Florence is very welcoming and helpful and will find you somewhere else to stay if she is full. She also runs the lovely **Old Sugar Mill Villa** nearby.

$$-$ Hot Rock Hostel, Salem, T664-491 9877, www.hotrockhostel.com. Member of the International Youth Hostel Federation, within walking distance of the MVO for students and backpackers, groups welcome, kitchen, living room, bunk beds.

❼ Restaurants

Montserrat *p61, map p64*

$$$ Hilltop Coffee House and Family Centre, Fogarthy Hill, T664-496 8765, see Facebook. David and Clover Lea, of **Gingerbread Hill** fame, have opened this café at the start of the Oriole Trail. One wall is devoted to the volcano, which David has filmed and photographed for years, another to album covers of musicians who recorded at Air Studios, and another to the late Arrow, see box, page 74. There is also a ping pong table, Wi-Fi, comfy seating and a balcony with ocean views. Good local juices, coffee or tea accompany pies, pastries and quiche.

$$$ Ziggy's Restaurant, Mahogany Loop, Woodlands, T664-491 8282, www.ziggysrestaurant.com. Dinner only, by reservation. Right on top of the hill overlooking Salem, the 2nd turning on the right from the main road. Dine by candlelight under canvas in cool gardens; the area is like parkland. Ziggy has been serving great food since the early 1990s: lobster quadrille, butterfly shrimp, jerk pork, chocolate sludge. Excellent wine list.

$$$-$$ Emerald Rose, St John's, T664-491 5941. Mon-Thu 0900-1900, Fri-Sat 0900-2030, dinner by reservation only. Local cuisine with weekend specials of goat water and souse.

$$$-$$ Gourmet Gardens, Olveston, T664-491 7859. Thu-Tue 1100-1400, 1800-2000. Approached up an alley way just below the Salem Police Station and set in lovely gardens, the restaurant is in a plantation-style outhouse with thick stone walls and a veranda. Dinner is by appointment only, so call ahead. Good food and good wines. Dutch-run, so more European dishes than Caribbean.

$$$-$$ JJ's Cuisine, Main Rd, St John's, T664-491 9024. Breakfast, lunch, sandwiches, snacks, takeaways, bar and dinner by reservation. A roadside restaurant just round the corner from **Tropical Mansions**, so guests come here to eat in preference to the hotel. It's a small, modern, purpose-built timber building, brightly painted with a veranda. The food is excellent and popular with locals for lunch, international cuisine.

$$$-$$ Oriole Café, Farara Plaza, Brades, next to the Tourist Board, T664-491 7144. Breakfast, lunch and dinner by reservation. Sit inside or outdoors overlooking Little Bay. West Indian food.

$$$-$$ Ponts Beach View, Little Bay, T664-496 7788, johnponteen@hotmail.co.uk. Lunch only. Views of the beach and cliffs, surrounded by plants. Food from the grill, chicken, fish, ribs, served with organic vegetables from the island and their own barbecue sauce. Wait for your food to be cooked with a lemonade and coconut chips on the deck overlooking the bay. Popular Sun barbecue.

$$$-$$ Tina's Restaurant, Brades Main Road, T664-491 3538. Lunch and dinner. Like many restaurants, this is a new wooden building in plantation style with a veranda, or you can eat inside with a/c. Very popular with locals, it is a good meeting place.

Local food such as chicken, fish and local vegetables, lobster burgers are popular and so is the coconut cream pie. Set back off the main road it has the best car park on Montserrat.

$$-$ The Attic, Olveston Estate Drive, just below the National Trust, T664-491 2008. Mon-Fri 0800-1600. Caters for the lunch crowd and popular for rotis and quesadillas. Also very good for local juices (guava, soursop, lime) and drinks such as ginger beer, tamarind or sorrel.

$$-$ Bitter End Beach Bar, Little Bay next to the ferry terminal, T664-491 3146. Open 0600-late. Seafood and snacks on the beach, lunch and dinner. Moose always seems to be open. Look out for his lobster special nights. Occasionally presents live bands from Antigua and the wider Caribbean.

$$-$ Morgan's Spotlight Bar, Sweeney's, T664-491 5419. Lunch. A snackette adjacent to the hospital, long established in an old rum shop type building, with the restaurant at the back of the bar. Local food, large portions, it is traditional to come here for Fri lunchtime to eat goat water. People travel miles for it.

$$-$ The People's Place, Fogarthy Hill, T664-491 8528. A roadside shack, next to **Hilltop Café**, painted bright blue, popular and friendly local lunch stop, eat indoors or outside if it isn't too windy on the hilltop, or takeaway. Limited choice but what you get is tasty, filling and plentiful. Good roti, goat water, fish, washed down with a cold Carib or rum and coconut water.

❶ Bars and clubs

Montserrat *p61, map p64*
Most of the bars and rum shops are in Little Bay, Cudjoe Head, Salem and St John's. They are small, forcing people outside to drink, 'lime' and play dominoes, staying open until the last guests leave. Fri night after work is the busiest night. Somewhere will have live music Fri, Sat nights, or at least a DJ, maybe from Antigua. Look out for the local entertainers, Pops Morris, Hero or Basil. The Tourist Board can give you details if a rum shop tour by van is scheduled. This takes you around a selection of local bars. If it isn't running, Salem has a collection of bars in close proximity for you to make your own pub crawl.

Bramble's, Cudjoe Head. A large bar where dominoes is the main activity.

Bunkum Bay Beach Bar, Bunkum Bay, T664-491 6077. Daily from 1200. A regular beach bar by day, offering fried chicken, pizza, burgers and cold drinks. Fri, Sat, Sun nights there are DJs. Sit indoors if you like it loud, or outside for a quieter time with waves breaking down below.

Da Club (Tony's), Salem, turn right after Rams Supermarket off the road heading to Old Towne. Latin music, very lively, doesn't start until after 2200 and goes on late.

Gary's Wide-awake Bar, Salem, T664-491 7156. One of the most popular late-night bars, often open after all the others close and remaining open as long as there are customers. An island institution and not to be missed.

Arrow

Alphonsus Cassell was born in Montserrat in 1949, one of nine children in a family brought up on music and calypso. Brothers Justin (aka Hero), and Lorenzo (aka Young Challenger), both won the Montserrat Calypso King. Alphonsus took the Junior Monarch crown in 1967, was runner-up to the Calypso King in 1969 and won the crown in 1970. He chose the stage name Arrow in honour of the Trinidadian calypsonion, the Mighty Sparrow. Arrow went on to win the contest three more times and make a name for himself in the wider Caribbean. After making his first recording, *Dance With Me, Woman*, in 1972, he moved to Trinidad and recorded the album *The Mighty Arrow On Target*. During the 1970s, calypso became more rhythmic and dance-oriented, in a style known as soca, an abbreviation of soul calypso. Arrow's style developed as an upbeat soca, his best known song being the ebullient *Hot Hot Hot* (1984), which spread like wildfire around the world in the 1980s, cementing his fame beyond the Caribbean. It was even chosen as the official anthem of the 1986 FIFA World Cup™, held in Mexico, has been used in eight movies or TV shows and is believed to have sold more than four million copies in various versions. In the 1980s and 1990s he toured the USA, Europe and Japan, and continued to record albums, more than 20 in total, incorporating other styles such as hip hop, zouk, merengue, R&B, salsa, even Latin brass and rock, and later house and rap.

On Montserrat, which remained his home, he set up a record company and a store, **Arrow's Manshop**, which he relocated to Salem in the north after the original store in Plymouth was destroyed by the volcano. In 2000 the Queen awarded him the MBE for services to Caribbean music. Further recognition came with an invitation to perform at the opening ceremony of the 2007 Cricket World Cup. His 2008 concert at the new Montserrat Cultural Centre was supposed to be his last, but he came out of retirement in 2010 to perform at a Haiti relief event there in 2010. Arrow died of cerebral cancer a few months later.

Good Life Night Club, Little Bay, T664-491 4576. On a hillside by the beach, plantation style with decking receiving a lovely sea breeze. Great disco for weekend dancing with a mixed clientele. Open for lunch 3-4 times a week, with a Caribbean-style buffet. The food is OK but it is a better bar than restaurant.
Jumping Jacks, Salem, T664-496 0574. Friendly bar, quite low key, relaxing music, snacks available.
Klub Supreme, Park St, Salem, T664-496 6275, Facebook.com/

klubsupreme01. 2200-late. Lots of special events including Christmas, New Year and St Patrick's Week. DJs from Antigua and elsewhere, Fri night is the best, when everything is a fiver.
Lord Hale's Bar, St John's, above **Anfa's Chinese Restaurant**. Friendly bar with live bands and dancing on high days and holidays.
The Lyme Sports Bar, Ryan's Court, Brades, T664-491 5559. Plasma screens for watching matches at the bar. Occasional live music when the atmosphere picks up after dark.
N&J's, Friths, Salem, T664-496 5723. Best on Fri nights when there is a barbecue, guest DJs and sometimes a band. Sit outside and watch the volcano in the distance.
Soca Cabana, Little Bay, T664-493 1820, www.socacabana.com. Beachside bar for drinks/food during the day with karaoke Sat night or live music weekends with dancing on the sand.
Treasure Spot Café, Cudjoe Head, T664-493 2003. Good place to come Fri night, often with live music which people listen to out on the road, 'liming' with friends in the evening air.

O Shopping

Montserrat *p61, map p64*
Arts and crafts
Arts & Crafts Association, Brades, near the Ministry of Agriculture, T664-496 1398. Mon-Fri 0900-1400. The association is very active and their outlet should not be missed for great handmade local souvenirs. Locally grown sea-island cotton, the green and yellow 'Madras' plaid cotton

used in the national dress, dolls, volcanic souvenirs, leather goods, local preserves, music and, of course, T-shirts are all good things to buy.
Oriole Gift Shop, National Trust, Salem, T664-491 3086. A good selection of local crafts.

Stamps
Montserrat Philatelic Bureau, Salem, same building as National Trust, T664-491 2042, www.montserratstamp bureau.com. Montserrat's postage stamps have traditionally been collectors' items. The island has issued its own stamps since 1876 and there are 6 issues a year and a definitive issue every 4-5 years. The volcanic eruption is featured, as is the eclipse of the sun.

O What to do

Montserrat *p61, map p64*
Birdwatching
At the **Montserrat National Trust**, Salem, T664-491 3086, www. montserratnationaltrust.ms, you can get an RSPB plastic card showing all the birds of Montserrat, together with a Nature Trails Map (EC$10). There is also a guide to the flora and fauna of the Centre Hills (EC$30) so you can explore the forests on your own, following the trails to spot the 34 species of birds resident on the island, including the endemic Montserrat oriole (*icterus oberi*), the national bird. Other species include the forest thrush, the bridled quail dove, the mangrove cuckoo, the trembler and the purple-throated carib. Birding guides arranged through the National

Trust cost US$25 for 1 person, US$20 per person for 2-3 people, US$15 per person for 4-5 people for up to 2 hrs. Longer tours are an extra US$10 per person per hr.

Scriber's Adventure Tours, Woodlands, T664-491 3412, http://scribersadventures.com. Birdwatching, bat watching (10 species on Montserrat), turtle watching and hiking. A former forest ranger with a keen interest in birds.

Cricket

First class cricket is played at the **Salem Cricket Ground**, and at the **Little Bay Playing Field.** Both have hosted regional cricket matches. Each weekend in Jan-Jun you can see local and regional cricket matches. **Montserrat Cricket Association**, Gregory Willock, T664-492 2770, mratcricket@gmail.com.

Cycling

Cycling on Montserrat is rewarding with lovely views, but be careful of fast drivers on twisty roads. Bikes can be rented from **David Lea**, Gingerbread Hill, T664-491 5812, www.volcano-island.com, or from **Imagine Peace Bicycle Shop**, Brades, T664-491 8809, ghbikes@hotmail.com.

Diving

Scuba Montserrat, Little Bay, T664-496 7807, www.scubamontserrat.com. Run by Andrew Myers and Emmy Aston, who provide courses, diving and snorkelling excursions, kayaking, beach picnics, volcano boat tours and equipment rental. PADI Open Water

certification US$600, 2-tank dive US$88, single-tank shore dive with guide US$35, snorkelling boat trip US$35 (equipment rental US$10), boat transfer to Rendezvous Bay US$15, round trip US$25, 2-seater inflatable kayaks, US$15 per hr.

Fishing

Several fishermen hire out their boats to take you deep-sea fishing or in shallow water. They catch marlin, wahoo, mahi mahi, king fish and tuna. Shore fishing is also popular on the west coast but be careful of standing too long in the sun. You can hire fishing rods from **N&B Service Centre**, Carr's Bay, T664-491 2575.

Bruce Farara, Olveston, T664-491 8802, farara@hotmail.com. Can take you fishing in a power boat.

Danny Sweeney, Olveston, T664-496 0574, mwilson@candw.ms. Long-time fisherman Danny Sweeney can take you fishing or organize watersports.

Football

There is a new FIFA-financed football ground at **Blakes**, in the north and football is played at weekends Jul-Dec. **Montserrat Football Association**, Vincent Cassell (President), Blakes Football Field, T664-491 8744, mfainc@candw.ms

Hiking

There are some excellent mountain walks in the north of the island. Contact **Montserrat National Trust**, T664-491 3086, as they maintain the trails and can advise you on guides. Hiking with a ranger is usually US$20

Diving around the volcano

The volcano has had an unexpected benefit for Montserrat's underwater life, as the three 4-km exclusion zones have created a marine reserve, with no one going into the area for some years. Pyroclastic flows chucked huge boulders into the sea off the south coast which formed new substrata for reefs. The waters are teeming with fish, coral and sponges and their larvae have drifted with the currents to the reefs of the north where the best dive sites are. Dive sites now stretch along 13 miles of coast from Old Road Bluff in the west to the tip of the island at North West Bluff and around the northeast to Hell's Gate, then down the east coast to the edge of the Maritime Exclusion Zone. Shore diving is good from **Lime Kiln Bay**, where there are ledges with coral, sponges and lots of fish; **Woodlands Bay**, where there is a shallow reef at 25 ft to 30 ft and a cave you can peep into to see coral banded shrimp and thousands of copper sweepers; at **Carr's Bay** where there are some excellent coral and interesting fish about 400 yds from the shore; and at Potato Hill reef just south of **Little Bay**, where there is wire coral, pillar coral, sea fans and black coral. **Rendezvous Bay** reef is one of the best for diving and at Rendezvous Bluff you can swim into the bat cave to see thousands of fruit bats hanging from the ceiling. Around the top of the island cliffs drop steeply to a sandy bottom at about 60 ft and here you can find schools of reef fish and pelagics, although there can also be strong currents. There are some shallow dives from boats, suitable for novices or a second dive, but also deep dives for experienced divers. **Pinnacle**, off the northeast coast, is a deep dive, dropping from 65 ft to 300 ft, where you can see amazing rock formations, brain coral, sponges and lots of fish. However, this side of the island, while offering dramatic underwater landscapes, is rarely dived because of rough seas.

per person depending on the size of the group, see Birdwatching, above.

Tour operators

Sightseeing can be arranged by boat around the southern end of Montserrat. Starting in Little Bay they head south to Plymouth, then round past the Tar River delta and up the east side to the old airport, giving you a different perspective on the pyroclastic flows and mudflows from the volcano, showing how the coastline has changed since 1995. Tours last 2 hrs and are dependent on weather and volcanic activity. Guides include: Danny Sweeney, see Fishing above; Hubert 'Buffy' Buffonge, Little Bay, T664-492 1570; or Lincoln 'Quan' Joseph, Brades, T664-496 2080.

There are also several tour operators based in Antigua or Montserrat which

operate day tours including volcano viewing, lunch and a tour of the island. **Carib World Travel**, Woods Centre, St John's, Antigua, T268-480 2999, www.carib-world.com.
Jenny Tours, Woods Centre, St John's, Antigua, T268-778 9786, www.jennytours.webs.com.
Ondeck, Falmouth Harbour, Antigua, T268-562 6696, www.ondeckocean racing.com/antigua/montserrat-adventure.htm. A 60-ft Farr ocean racing yacht departs Falmouth Harbour at 0800, arriving in Little Bay at 1200, returning 1300 and arriving back in Falmouth Harbour at 1800, US$189. You can opt to stay in Montserrat overnight or longer.
RTT Travel & Tours, Brades, Montserrat, T664-491 4788, www.rtttravelandtours.com.
Runaway Travel, Brades, Montserrat, T664-491 2776, runaway@candw.ms.

⊖ Transport

Montserrat *p61, map p64*
Air
John A Osborne Airport has a 600-m (1968-ft) runway which can handle small planes. There is also a helipad.

Car hire
With a valid driving licence, you can obtain a local 3-month licence (EC$50/US$20) at the police station in Salem, or at Police HQ in Brades. **Be-Peep's Car Rentals**, Olveston, T664-491 3787, for cars and jeeps; **Equipment & Supplies Ltd**, Olveston, T664-491 2402, for cars and vans; **Ethelyne's Car Rental**, Olveston, T664-491 2855; **KC's Car Rentals**, Olveston, T664-491 5756, kccarrental@hotmail. com; **Montserrat Enterprises Ltd**, Old Towne, T664-491 2431, melenter@ candw.ms; **MS Osborne Ltd**, Brades, T664-491 2494, msosborne@candw. ms; **Pickett's Rentals**, Salem, T664-491 5513, johnsonwp@candw.ms; **Zeekies Rentals**, Baker Hill, T664-491 4515.

Taxi
There are dozens of taxis offering transport and tours; ask the Tourist Board for recommendations.

⊙ Directory

Montserrat *p61, map p64*
Medical services Glendon Hospital is in St John's, for most routine and surgical emergencies, T664-491 2552. Private doctors/dentist also available. Serious medical cases are taken by helicopter to Antigua or Guadeloupe.

Contents

Footprint features

The islands of St Kitts (officially named St Christopher) and Nevis are in the north part of the Leeward Islands. Slightly off the beaten track, neither island is overrun with tourists; St Kitts is developing its southern peninsula where there are sandy beaches, but most of the island is untouched. Rugged volcanic peaks, forests and old fortresses produce spectacular views, and hiking is very rewarding. Two miles away, the conical island of Nevis is smaller and very desirable. Plantation houses on both islands have been converted into some of the most romantic hotels in the Caribbean, very popular with honeymooners. While one federation, the sister islands are quite different. St Kitts, the larger, is more cosmopolitan and lively, receiving international flights and the largest cruise ships, while Nevis is quieter and more sedate, receiving regional flights and smaller craft. Wherever you go on these two small islands there are breathtaking, panoramic views of the sea, mountains, cultivated fields and small villages.

Fauna and flora on St Kitts and Nevis

Both islands are home to the green vervet monkey, introduced by the French 300 years ago. They can be seen in many areas including Brimstone Hill but can be a pest to farmers. To keep down numbers, many have been exported for medical research. The monkey is the same animal as on Barbados but the Kittitians used to eat them. Another animal, the mongoose, imported to kill rats and snakes, never achieved its original purpose (rats being nocturnal whereas the mongoose is active by day). It has, however, contributed to the extinction of many species of lizard, ground-nesting birds, green iguanas, brown snakes and red-legged tortoises. There are some wild deer on the southeast peninsula, imported in the 1930s from Puerto Rico. In common with other West Indian islands, there are highly vocal frogs, lizards (the anole is the most common), fruit bats, insect bats and butterflies. Birds typical of the region include brown pelicans, frigate birds and three species of hummingbird.

St Kitts and Nevis are small islands, yet have a wide variety of habitats, with rainforest, dry woodland, wetland, grassland and salt ponds. The forests on the sister islands are restricted in scale, but provide a habitat for wild orchids, candlewoods and exotic vines. Fruits and flowers, both wild and cultivated, are in abundance, particularly in the gorgeous gardens of Nevis. Trees include several varieties of the stately royal palm, the spiny-trunked sandbox tree, silk-cotton tree, and the turpentine or gum tree.

St Kitts → *For listings, see pages 102-116.*

St Kitts is made up of three groups of rugged volcano peaks split by deep ravines and a low-lying peninsula in the southeast where there are salt ponds and fine beaches. The dormant volcano, Mount Liamuiga (1156 m, 3792 ft, pronounced Lie-a-mee-ga) occupies the central part of the island. The mountain was previously named Mount Misery by the British, but has now reverted to its Carib name, meaning 'fertile land'. The foothills of the mountains, particularly in the north, are covered with sugar cane plantations and grassland, while the uncultivated lowland slopes are covered with forest and fruit trees. St Kitts was the last 'sugar island' in the Leewards group, but the industry operated at a loss and finally closed in 2005. Evidence of sugar cane is everywhere on the comparatively flat, fertile coastal plain. You will drive through large fields of cane and glimpse the narrow-gauge railway that was used to transport it from the fields. Disused sugar mills are also often seen. Around the island are the

Great Houses: Fairview, Clay Villa, Romney Manor (destroyed by fire in 1995), the White House (closed), Golden Lemon (closed), Rawlins (closed), Lodge (closed) and Ottley's, not all of which are open to the public. The decline in the sugar industry has thrown St Kitts into the arms of the tourist industry instead. Basseterre, and St Kitts in general, is heavily dependent on cruise ship tourism. All the shops, arcades and stalls open when a ship is in port and the place is lively and vibrant, yet everything can seem dead and dull when there isn't. If you like to have the place to yourself, time your excursions according to the cruise ship schedule, copies of which are held by most hotels.

St Kitts

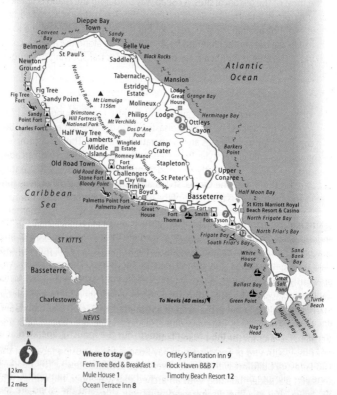

Where to stay
Fern Tree Bed & Breakfast 1
Mule House 1
Ocean Terrace Inn 8
Ottley's Plantation Inn 9
Rock Haven B&B 7
Timothy Beach Resort 12

Arriving in St Kitts

Getting there Long-haul flights arrive from the UK and North America directly into St Kitts, some of which are seasonal, but otherwise you have to fly to a neighbouring island such as Puerto Rico and change planes. Cruise ships call at St Kitts, but links by boat with other islands are few and informal.

Getting around Buses are cheap and speedy. Drivers are generally very obliging and, if asked, may even divert their route to accommodate you. They run from very early in the morning until 2300. Buses are identified by their green H registration plate, flag them down with a wave. **Cars**, jeeps and mini mokes can be hired from a variety of agencies. Driving is on the left. The main road on St Kitts is, for the most part, very good and motorists, especially bus drivers, can drive very fast. A clockwise route around the island will enable you to see most of the historical sites. A cheap way of touring the island is to take a minibus from Basseterre (Bay Road) to Dieppe Bay Town, then walk to Saddlers (there might be a minibus if you are lucky, but it is only half a mile up the road) where you can get another minibus back to Basseterre along the Atlantic coast. Parking in Basseterre is difficult. For details of **ferries** transporting passengers between St Kitts and Nevis see page 115.

Basseterre

The port of Basseterre is the capital and largest town, founded in 1727. Earthquakes, hurricanes and finally a disastrous fire destroyed the town in 1867 and consequently its buildings are comparatively modern. There is a complete mishmash of architectural styles from elegant Georgian buildings with arcades, verandas and jalousies, mostly in good condition, to hideous 20th-century concrete block houses. The **Circus**, styled after London's Piccadilly Circus (but looking nothing like it), is the centre of the town. It is busiest on Friday afternoon and comes alive with locals 'liming' (relaxing). The clock tower is a memorial to Thomas Berkeley, former president of the General Legislative Council. The development of tourism has meant a certain amount of redevelopment in the centre. An old warehouse on the waterfront has been converted into the Pelican Mall, a duty-free shopping and recreational complex. It also houses the Ministry of Tourism and a lounge for guests of the **Four Seasons Resort** in Nevis awaiting transport. The cruise ship berth on the waterfront is between Bramble Street and College Street in the heart of Basseterre, capable of accommodating the largest ships afloat, together with a sailing and power boat marina, and berthing facilities for the inter-island ferries.

At the south end of Fort Street on Bay Road is the imposing façade of the **Old Treasury Building**, with a dome covering an arched gateway. This building replaced a wooden building with an arched gateway, once the entrance to the town after you had disembarked from your ship at Treasury Pier. It was built in 1894 and the construction was financed by unused deposits on return voyages for indentured Portuguese labourers, most of whom chose to stay on the island rather than return at the end of their contract. It has been converted into the **National Museum**, and also houses the **St Christopher National Trust** ① *T869-465 5584, www.stkittsheritage.com, Mon, Tue, Thu and Fri 0830-1300, 1400-1600, Wed and Sat, 0830-1300, US$3* (formerly the St Christopher Heritage Society), which has a small, interesting display of old photographs and artefacts together with other exhibits of national culture and arts. They work on conservation projects and are grateful for donations.

Head north up Fort Street, turn left at the main thoroughfare (Cayon Street) and you will come to **St George's church**, set in its own large garden, with a massive, square buttressed tower. The site was originally a Jesuit church, Notre Dame, which was razed to the ground by the English in 1706. Rebuilt four years later and renamed St George's, it suffered damage from hurricanes and

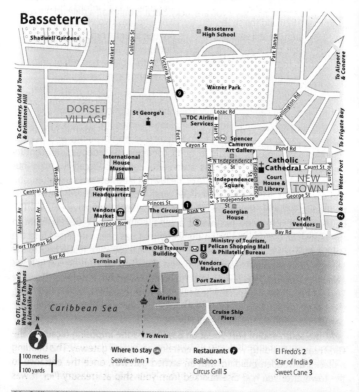

Basseterre

Shadwell Gardens
Basseterre High School
Market St
College St
Nevis St
Victoria Rd
Park Range
To Airport & Conaree

To Cemetery, Old Rd Town & Brimstone Hill
DORSET VILLAGE
Warner Park ⑨
St George's ✝
Fort St
Lozac Rd
TDC Airline Services ♪
Hart St
Spencer Cameron Art Gallery
Cayon St
Wellington Rd
Pond Rd
To Frigate Bay

International House Museum 🏛
Church St
N Independence St
Catholic Cathedral
Caunt St
Pitt St

Government Headquarters
N Independence Sq
Independence Square
S Independence St
Court House & Library
NEW TOWN
George St
To 2 & Deep Water Port

Westbourne St
Central St
Malone Av
Durant St
Princes St
The Circus ❶
Bank St
Georgian House ❶
Craft Vendors

Vendors Market
Liverpool Row
$
Bay Rd

Fort Thomas Rd
❺
Bay Rd
The Old Treasury Building
Ministry of Tourism, Pelican Shopping Mall & Philatelic Bureau
Bus Terminal
Vendors Market ❸
Port Zante

Caribbean Sea
Marina
⛵

To OTI, Fisherman's Wharf, Fort Thomas & Limekiln Bay
N
Cruise Ship Piers
▼ To Nevis

100 metres
100 yards

Where to stay 🛏	Restaurants 🍴	El Fredo's **2**
Seaview Inn **1**	Ballahoo **1**	Star of India **9**
	Circus Grill **5**	Sweet Cane **3**

Kim Collins, the Quiet Man

Market Street is the home of Kim Collins, the sprinter who won the 100 m in 9.98 seconds at the Commonwealth Games in Manchester in 2002 and again in 10.07 seconds at the World Track and Field Championships in Paris in 2003. After his Paris triumph, St Kitts honoured him by naming a highway after him, putting his image on a postage stamp, giving him a diplomatic passport and a house worth US$150,000. 25 August was named Kim Collins Day.

Born in 1976 and the sixth of 11 children, he still spends three months of the year in St Kitts, where he is treated as a national hero. The rest of the time he lives in the USA, where he graduated in sociology from Texas Christian University, in Fort Worth. Collins represented St Kitts at the summer Olympics four times from 1996 to 2008 and competed at eight consecutive World Championships from 1997 to 2011. He was due to run in the 2012 London Olympics but was dropped by the St Kitts Olympic officials after he had an unsanctioned meeting with his wife at a hotel, missing training sessions.

Collins continues to run. In July 2013 he set a new personal and national record for the 100 m with a time of 9.97 seconds in Lausanne, a time which equalled the Masters M35 age division world record of Linford Christie when he was two years younger. A week later he ran the 100 m in Budapest in a time of 9.99 seconds, the sixth time he had run in under 10 seconds and becoming the oldest man (aged 37 years three months and five days) to run that distance at that speed. In February 2014 he smashed another Masters M35 world record when he ran the indoor 60 m in 6.49 seconds.

earthquakes on several occasions. It, too, was a victim of the 1867 fire. It was rebuilt in 1869 and contains some attractive stained-glass windows. Further hurricane damage since the end of the 1980s has led to ongoing repair works. There is a fine view of the town from the tower.

Independence Square was built in 1790 and is surrounded now by a low white fence; eight gates let paths converge on a fountain in the middle of the square (it looks like the Union Jack when seen from the air). There are gaily painted muses on top of the fountain. Originally designed for slave auctions and council meetings and called Pall Mall Square, it was renamed after independence in 1983 and now contains many plants, spacious lawns and lovely old trees. It is surrounded by 18th-century houses and, at its east end, the **Roman Catholic Cathedral** with its twin towers. Built in 1927, the Immaculate Conception is surprisingly plain inside. The first Catholic church was built in 1856 after an influx of Portuguese from Madeira after 1835 increased demand for services and this is its replacement. At 10 North Square Street you can visit the very attractive building housing the **Spencer Cameron Art Gallery** ① *T869-664 4157, see Facebook, also a gallery at the Marriott*. See Rosey Cameron-Smith's paintings and prints of local views and customs, as well as an impressive selection of work by other artists. On West Independence Square, the **Court House** reflects the old one which burnt down in 1867. It is an impressive building in the colonial style. The **Bank of Nova Scotia** houses some interesting paintings of Brimstone Hill by Lt Lees of the Royal Engineers, circa 1783. On South Square Street is one of the best examples of 18th-century English colonial architecture, known as **Georgian House**. It probably once held slaves in its cellars, either prior to or post auction before being transferred to the plantations. It was built at the end of the 18th century and in the mid-19th century it was the home of a thriving merchant, James Berridge, whose fleet traded throughout the Caribbean and up the eastern seaboard of the USA and Canada. He was also Treasurer of the island's government, Lt Colonel of the Windward Regiment of Foot and Aide de Camp to the Governor. The **International House Museum and Edgar Challenger Library** ① *Central St, T869-465 0542, Mon-Fri 1000-1700, Sat 1000-1300, Sun 1300-1700. US$5 for visitors, US$1.85 for locals*, was designed by Winston Zack Nisbett, a cultural preservationist and friend of the previous owner of the property, Edgar Challenger, a well-known trade unionist and historian, who died in 2001. Challenger's small, wooden residence was a gold mine of traditional utensils and equipment used between 1920 and 1940, as well as books on the history of the Federation and other papers and records, some of which go back to the early 17th century.

West coast

The west coast overlooking the Caribbean Sea is guarded by no less than nine **forts** and the magnificent Brimstone Hill Fortress. Taking the road out of Basseterre, you will pass the sites of seven of them: Fort Thomas, Palmetto Point Fort, Stone Fort, Fort Charles, Charles Fort, Sandy Point Fort and Fig Tree Fort. The remaining two are to the south of Basseterre: Fort Smith and Fort Tyson. Little remains of any of them.

Heading west from Basseterre along the Caribbean coast, you come to the village of **Boyd's** and the newly restored and rebuilt **Fairview Great House** ① *T869-465 3141, http://fairviewstkitts.com, daily 0900-1700, US$10 for day visit, US$5 for 1-hr tour, children free*. Built in 1701 for a French army commanding officer, it was surrounded by a wall with a gun emplacement at the edge of the property, a feature not seen at plantation houses inland nor on the east coast. The house has had a variety of owners and in the late 20th century was known as a comfortable hotel, the Fairview Inn, when it was converted and expanded in 1968. However, its fortunes declined at the turn of the millennium and the hotel closed. In 2008 it changed hands again and repairs commenced to try to

Defence of the realm

Sir Thomas Warner landed at Old Road Bay in 1623 and was joined in 1625 by the crew of a French ship badly mauled by the Spanish. They were initially befriended by the local chief Tegreman, but the Kalinago (Caribs) became alarmed at the rapid colonization of the island. Tegreman called in reinforcements from other islands and 3000 Caribs tried to mount an attack in 1626. However, in a pre-emptive strike, 2000 of them were massacred by the combined French and English forces at Bloody Point (the site of Stone Fort). This marked the end of Kalinago occupation of the island as the survivors were deported to Waitukubuli (Dominica).

An amicable settlement between the French and English in 1627 meant that the English held the central portion of the island roughly in line from Sandy Point to Saddlers in the north to Bloody Point across to Cayon in the south.

A large tamarind tree at Half Way Tree marked one of the boundaries. French names can be traced in both of their areas of influence (Dieppe Bay Town in the north, the parishes are called Capisterre and Basseterre in the south). The southeast peninsula was neutral. Both French and English used St Kitts as a base for colonizing other islands: Antigua, Montserrat and Nevis for the English, with Sir Thomas Warner appointed Governor of St Christopher, Nevis, Barbados and Montserrat in 1925, and the French settling Martinique, Guadeloupe and Saint-Barthélemy. This rapprochement did not last long as, following the colonization of Martinique and Guadeloupe, the French wished to increase their sphere of influence. St Kitts became a target and in 1664 they squeezed the English from the island. For 200 years the coast was defended by troops from one nation or another.

restore historical features with accuracy. It is now open to the public for tours, popular with cruise ship visitors, there is a restaurant which is good for tea after a tour of the island, rum tasting, a swimming pool and botanical gardens are being developed.

Another plantation house on the island tour itineraries is **Clay Villa** ⓘ *Challengers Village, Trinity Palmetto Point, T869-465 2353, www.clayvilla.com, tours by appointment.* The 1763 house and gardens covering 10 acres are a family home, but there is a small museum and the owners give a very informative tour followed by a delicious rum or fruit punch. There is an emphasis on the Amerindian heritage, partly because this was a free working estate which never used African slaves. Profits from tours go towards local good causes, mainly animal welfare. Many of the beneficiaries, such as a one-legged parrot and several dogs can be seen in the grounds, together with other wildlife.

The Sugar Train

The sugar industry was revolutionized in St Kitts when first the estates moved from wind to steam power in 1870 and then a central sugar factory was built in Basseterre in 1912. A narrow-gauge railway was built in 1912-1926 to deliver cane from the fields to the central sugar mill and it was the beginning of the end for all the small estate-based sugar mills dotted around the island. Many sail-less windmills still stand as relics of the old ways. Although the track initially ran as two spurs either side of the island, planters soon saw the sense of abandoning other delivery systems and it was extended to be a circular route all round the coast. With the decline in the sugar industry at the end of the 20th century, the track fell into disrepair but has now been renovated with new rails and bridges by the company running the tourist train, for the added benefit of the sugar company. The St Kitts Scenic Railway, which opened in 2003, is the perfect way to see the whole island, far better than touring by car as you get a much better view. The railway is mostly uphill from the road, although in many places it runs along the coast, and with the double decker carriages you are above vegetation which blocks your view from a car.

The locomotive originated in Romania but was sold to Poland for sugar beet transport before coming to St Kitts for sugar cane. The power car was built in Colorado, USA, while the 'island series' carriages, the first of their kind, were built in Seattle, Washington, USA. The rails were brought from the UK, Belgium, the USA and abandoned sugar track in Cuba, the sleepers are hard wood from Guyana. An Alaskan engineer is always on board to answer questions and a Kittitian choir will serenade you.

St Kitts Scenic Railway departs from Needsmust station near the airport, three hours 10 minutes, but only when there is a cruise ship in port. It is expensive, at US$89 per adult, US$44.50 per child. An alternative would be to do a partial journey with a tour of Brimstone Hill Fortress for US$123, returning to the starting point by bus. A maximum of 28 guests per carriage have a seat on both levels, the upper open-air deck and the lower, enclosed, air-conditioned carriage. Reservations essential, T869-465 7263, www.stkittsscenicrailway.com.

At Old Road Town turn right to visit **Romney Manor** and the Wingfield Estate. As you approach, the remains of the island's Amerindian civilization can be seen on large stones with drawings and petroglyphs. Romney Manor was bought by the Earl of Romney at the beginning of the 17th century and was one of the most important sugar producers on the island. It is believed that the

Carib chief, Tegreman, previously had his village on what are now the grounds of the house. In 1834 the Romney Estate was the first to emancipate its slaves, despite contrary instructions from the British Parliament. Unfortunately, Romney Manor was destroyed by fire in 1995, but the gardens remain with views over the coast. There is an enormous saman tree, believed to date from around 1600-1650, which has a girth of 20 feet and a span of a quarter of an acre. Romney Manor is now home to **Caribelle Batik** ① *Mon-Fri, 0830-1600, T869-465 6253, www.caribellebatikstkitts.com*, which has a well-stocked shop and you can watch the artists producing the colourful and highly attractive material. A guide will explain the process.

Adjacent to Romney Manor is **Wingfield Estate**, where you can see the remains of old sugar machinery and buildings, including a 17th-century rum distillery, the only aqueduct on the island. There are also ongoing archaeological digs which can be viewed. The estate dates from 1625 and was the first land granted in the English West Indies. Initially it grew tobacco and indigo, but from 1640 onwards it concentrated on sugar and rum. As technology developed, sugar was crushed first by animal power, then water power and eventually a steam engine, evidence of which can all be seen. Tour guides are available if you wish, but there are display boards you can read so they aren't essential. There is a café, gift shop and toilets. Wingfield Estate is also the home of **Sky Safari** ① *T869-466 4259, www.skysafaristkitts.com, reservations essential, cruise passengers are not allowed to book independently and have to do it through their ship's excursion programme*, a zipline excursion through the rainforest with stunning views over the island down to Brimstone Hill Fortress and the sea. There is a short training line, then you are taken up the mountain in an open-air truck (look for green vervet monkeys along the way), from where you harness up for three breathtaking traverses across a small valley, followed by a double line race to the end. Staff are friendly, entertaining and safety-conscious, but guests always wish there were more runs.

If you keep driving to the left of Romney Manor and **Caribelle Batik**, you will find one of the highest paved roads on the island. It is a tough climb so only attempt it if you have a sturdy car. A large flat rock at the top is a perfect spot to admire the view. To the right is a smaller path that leads to an incredible overview of Bat Hole Ghaut. The views of tropical rainforest in myriad greens are magnificent. You can reach the attractive but secluded **Dos d'Ane Pond** near **Mount Verchilds** from the Wingfield Estate; a guide is recommended.

At the village of **Middle Island**, you will see, on your right and slightly up the hill, the church of St Thomas at the head of an avenue of dead or dying royal palms. Here is buried Sir Thomas Warner who died on 10 March 1649. The raised tomb under a canopy is inscribed 'General of y Caribee'. There is also a bronze plaque with a copy of the inscription inside the church. Other early tombs are of Captain John Pogson (1656) and Sir Charles Payne, 'Major General of Leeward Carribee Islands', who was buried in 1744. The tower, built in 1880, fell during earth tremors in 1974.

Brimstone Hill

ⓘ T869-465 2609, www.brimstonehillfortress.org, daily 0930-1730, entry US$10 for foreigners, US$2.30 for nationals, children half price; allow up to 2 hrs. The local minibus to Brimstone Hill is US$2, then walk up to the fortress (less than 30 mins but extremely steep; for fit climbers only).

The **Brimstone Hill Fortress National Park**, one of the 'Gibraltars of the West Indies' (a title it shares with Les Saintes, off Guadeloupe), sprawls over 38 acres on the slopes of a hill 800 ft above the sea. It commands an incredible view of St Kitts and Nevis and on clear days you can see Anguilla (67 miles), Montserrat (40 miles), Saba (20 miles), St Eustatius (five miles), St Barts (40 miles) and St Martin (45 miles). It was inaugurated as a national park by Queen Elizabeth II in October 1985 and gained UNESCO World Heritage Site status in October 2000. The English mounted the first cannon on Brimstone Hill in 1690 in an attempt to force the French from Fort Charles below and the fortress was not abandoned until 1852. It has been constructed mainly out of local volcanic stones and was designed along classic defensive lines. The five bastions overlook each other and also guard the only road as it zigzags up to the parade ground. The entrance is at the Barrier Redan where payment is made. Pass the Magazine Bastion but stop at the Orillon Bastion which contains the massive ordnance store (165 ft long with walls at least 6 ft thick). The hospital was located here and under the south wall is a small cemetery. You then arrive at the Prince of Wales Bastion (note the graffitied name of J Sutherland, 93rd Highlanders 24 October 1822 on the wall next to one of the cannon) from where there are good views over to the parade ground. Park at the parade ground, there is a small snack bar and good gift shop near the warrant officer's quarters with barrels of pork outside it. Stop for a good video introduction at the DL Matheson Visitor Centre. A narrow and quite steep path leads to Fort George, the Citadel and the highest defensive position. Restoration is continuing and several areas have been converted to form a most interesting museum. Barrack rooms now hold well-presented and informative displays (pre-Columbian, American, English, French and Garrison). Guides are on hand to give more detailed explanations of the fortifications.

Beyond Brimstone Hill at Sandy Point is the relatively new attraction, **Amazing Grace Experience** ⓘ Crab Hill, Sandy Point, T869-465 1122, www.amazinggraceexperience.com, Mon-Sat 0900-1700, Sun 0915-1300, US$5, children under 12 free, opened in 2012 honouring the man who wrote the lyrics to Amazing Grace. John Newton (1725-1807), a slave trader, became a reformed man during a visit to St Kitts in 1754. He subsequently joined the clergy, became actively involved in the abolitionist movement and wrote

Hiking

St Kitts has comparatively clear trails including Old Road to Philips, the old British military road, which connected the British settlements on the northeast and southwest coasts without going through French territory when the island was partitioned. There are also trails from Belmont to the crater of Mount Liamuiga, from Saddlers to the Peak, from Lamberts or the top of Wingfield Heights to Dos d'Ane pond. There are excellent hiking tours to the volcano and through the rainforest.

several hymns with the poet William Cowper, including *Amazing Grace*. It was written to illustrate a sermon on New Year's Day 1773, nearly 20 years after his visit to the island. The music most closely associated with the hymn, *New Britain*, was not added until 1835. It is a small but interesting exhibition which does its best to link the hymn to St Kitts.

Mount Liamuiga

The island is dominated by the southeast range of mountains (1159 ft) and the higher northwest range which contains **Mount Verchilds** (2931 ft) and the crater of **Mount Liamuiga** (3792 ft). To climb Mount Liamuiga independently, get a bus to St Paul's. Just after the village entrance sign there is a track leading through farm buildings which you follow through the fields. After 20 minutes take a left fork. At the edge of the forest, the track becomes a path, which is easy to follow and leads through wonderful trees; on the steady climb from the end of the road note the wild orchids in the forest. If you hear something in the upper branches, look up before the monkeys disappear. The green vervet monkey was introduced by the French some 300 years ago and Kittitians used to eat them. They can be seen in many areas including Brimstone Hill but can be a pest to farmers. To keep down numbers, many have been exported for medical research.

The last half a mile is a bit of a scramble, with rocks and tree roots and it is very steep and slippery. At 2600 ft is the crater, which is where guides usually end the hike, giving you a 10-minute photo opportunity before heading back down again. Only fit hikers should attempt this hike as it is strenuous. It can be done by experienced walkers in 1½ hours, although if you go with a guide it will take two hours, stopping to look at interesting flora and fauna along the way. If you are a slow walker not used to hills, arrange a private guide who can go at your pace; people often turn round before the top because they can't keep up with the group's pace. Downhill can often be as hard as uphill. Wear proper hiking shoes or boots, be prepared to get dirty and maybe take walking sticks as well as a small backpack with water and a snack. It is possible to climb down into the crater if you are not in a tour party, holding on to vines and roots, but to get beyond the crater to the summit you need a guide and this will be an all-day trip.

North coast

There is a black-sand beach at **Dieppe Bay**. The beach has been moved around by hurricanes but it is still a good place to stroll, with lots of sandpipers and herons and a view of The Quill on St Eustatius in the distance. Pass through Saddlers to the **Black Rocks**. Here lava has flowed into the sea, providing interesting rock formations. The main road continues southeast along the Atlantic coast. At **Lodge Village** there is a fine 18th-century Great House in tropical gardens overlooking the sea. Built by Samuel Crooke, a fourth generation Kittitian, sugar planter and member of the Island Council, it is currently under new ownership and awaiting conversion to a Heritage Tourism Attraction. Close by is **Ottleys Plantation Inn**, an 1832 Great House now a luxury hotel and a beautiful and atmospheric place to go for lunch or dinner if you aren't staying there. The road then continues through Cayon (turn right uphill to Spooners for a look at the abandoned Cotton Ginnery, built in 1901 and operated until the 1970s) back to Basseterre via the RL Bradshaw Airport.

Southeast peninsula

The southeast spit of land, the tail of the tadpole that is St Kitts, is where you find the island's sandy beaches and salt ponds. Until very recently, this was a remote area frequented by more goats than people, but now it is accessible for all. There are also some wild deer, imported originally from Puerto Rico in the 1930s, and the green vervet monkey can often be seen. To visit the southeast peninsula, turn off the roundabout at the end of Wellington Road (opposite the turning to the airport) and at the end of this new road turn left. This leads to the narrow spit of land sandwiched between North and South Frigate Bays. The six-mile Dr Kennedy A Simmonds Highway runs from Frigate Bay to Major's Bay along the backbone of the peninsula and around the salt pond. From the top there is a lookout with a great view of North Friars Bay Beach on the Atlantic and South Friars Bay Beach on the Caribbean Sea, with Nevis at the end. This area is being gradually developed as a 2500-acre luxury resort, **Christophe Harbour**. Already in operation are a beach club, beach restaurant and several villas, while a **Hyatt** hotel is under construction, as is a marina capable of accommodating super-yachts and a Tom Fazio-designed golf course.

Frigate Bay Frigate Bay is now dominated by the huge **Marriott Hotel** on the north (Atlantic) side and adjacent golf course and condominiums. Breakers have been built so that guests can get into the water and a reef gives the rest of the bay some protection, but generally beaches on the Atlantic side are not safe for swimming. The sand is kept clean by staff at the Marriott, even beyond the property's boundaries. **South Frigate Bay** is on the Caribbean Sea and is popular with locals and students from Ross University as it is the closest beach to the capital and has a string of beach bars collectively known as 'The Strip'. Consequently it isn't the cleanest beach on the island and the beach loungers are shabby, but it is pleasant and there is good snorkelling around the rocks in front of the **Timothy Beach Resort**. If the sea is a bit rough, watch out for rocks when entering the water but once you get out a bit further there is sand underfoot. Friday night is the night to come for partying and dancing on the beach. Keep an eye on your drinks when on the beach, as the green vervet monkeys are likely to steal them. Some like non-alcoholic drinks but there are lots that are partial to alcohol, apparently a habit picked up years ago by eating fermenting sugar cane in the fields. They get drunk, they fall over and sometimes they fight. Just like people.

Friars Bay **North Friars Bay** beach is very open and sandy but swimming is dangerous. There are no facilities, no shade and no beach bar. Access is best at the far end. **South Friars Bay** is a long stretch of sand with access at the north and south ends. Take the right fork in the track to the north end, where there are beach bars and nice sand which is cleaned regularly. What appear to be shacks quickly spring into life as bars according to demand, such as when a cruise ship is in port and it can get very busy at weekends. Two sunbeds and an umbrella rent for US$10. The left fork leads to the southern end and **Shipwreck Beach Bar**, open 1000-sundown. There are some grungy old sunloungers to rent on the beach and a portacabin toilet as well as scruffy thatched umbrellas for shade. The sand here is quite dark and the beach is changing shape because of storms. There is a step down into the water and a platform you can swim to offshore where snorkelling is good (snorkelling gear for rent). Pelicans dive for fish and the view of cliffs and mountains is attractive. Keep an eye out for monkeys in this area.

White House Bay White House Bay, on the Caribbean side is good for snorkelling, but unfortunately a hurricane took away a lot of the sand. It is a popular anchorage for yachts and a great dive site with wrecks in the bay. Archaeological research is taking place underwater. The Anglo-Danish Maritime Archaeological Team (ADMAT) set up a field school in 2003, the largest of this sort ever carried out in the Caribbean. The aim is to record two pre-1760s ship wrecks uncovered by recent hurricanes.

Sand Bank Bay The road down the peninsula skirts the Great Salt Pond. Halfway round the pond turn left down an unmarked dirt road to reach Sand Bank Bay, a lovely secluded beach. Park near the road and walk the short distance to the beach. The bay is horseshoe-shaped backed by sand dunes with hills at each end. There are no public facilities, although a few houses have been built, set back from the beach and there is a private beach club at one end, **The Pavilion**, part of the Christophe Harbour development, but otherwise it is just a wild, windy and empty beach apart from a few cows. Kite flying is good and it's a great place for picnics, but don't swim, there is an undertow and drownings have occurred.

Cockleshell Bay Continue on the main highway and turn left for Cockleshell Bay and Turtle Beach. Cockleshell Beach is a two-mile curving stretch of sand, the closest point to Nevis and with a stunning view across the water. The bay is scheduled for development and if you walk west around the point you will see the grand new **Hyatt** hotel being built on Banana Bay. In the meantime there are just a few beach bars, from the gourmet **Spice Mill Restaurant** with its luxury sunbeds, through the **Lion Rock Beach Bar**, known for its ice-cold beer and a mean rum punch, to the barbecue-style **Reggae Beach Bar**, with power boats moored offshore. You can hire sunbeds and snorkelling gear and head for the rocks, where there are lots of colourful fish. Sometimes seaweed litters the sand and sometimes large rollers provide surf to play in, but there is a gentle slope and the water doesn't get deep very quickly. Women offer aloe vera massages on the beach, which can be a bit of a nuisance if you don't want one, but great if you do. The beach comes to life for special occasions in high season, sometimes for cruise ship visitors, and is popular with Kittitians at weekends. On a weekday in summer, however, you'll have the place to yourself. A taxi from Basseterre costs about US$26 and from Frigate Bay US$22.

Turtle Beach Turtle Beach on Mosquito Bay is a quiet public beach, like all beaches on St Kitts and Nevis, so don't be put off by the gate and fence before you get to the sand. Swimming is good here, as is snorkelling, protected by a reef. There is a very elegant bar and restaurant, **The Beach House**, part of Christophe Harbour, which is only open for parties and functions, and a jetty for motorboats. Weed comes in if the wind is in the wrong direction and is cleaned off the sand fairly haphazardly, but at least the worst is removed. You can get a water taxi to Nevis from here.

Major's Bay The main road ends at Major's Bay, which is a thin strip of land between the sea and the pond. The sand is mostly at the far end and it is rocky where the cars stop. The sea bridge ferry between St Kitts and Nevis for vehicles comes in very near here. There is an old barge in the bay and a lovely view of Nevis. The barge was used during the construction of the cruise ship pier and during a hurricane it was brought here for shelter, but it was wrecked on the shore. It is now a breeding ground for fish. The water is calm and there is nothing here apart from the occasional animal.

Banana Bay Banana Bay is next to Cockleshell Bay with fine sand and good bathing and a lovely view of Nevis. There was once a hotel here, the Banana Bay Beach Hotel, but it was destroyed in 1998 in a hurricane. Now it is the location for the new Hyatt hotel under construction, part of the 2500-acre resort community, Christophe Harbour, being developed on the peninsula.

Nevis → *For listings, see pages 102-116.*

Across the two-mile Narrows Channel from St Kitts is the beautiful little island of Nevis. The circular island covers an area of 36 sq miles and the central peak, 3232 ft, is usually shrouded in white clouds and mist. It reminded Columbus of Spanish snow-capped mountains and so he called the island 'Las Nieves'. For the Kalinago (Caribs), it was Oualie, the land of beautiful water. Smaller than St Kitts, it is also quieter. The atmosphere is low-key and easy-going; all the same, it is an expensive island. The delightful plantation inns have long been a favourite with the well-heeled British but the construction of the Four Seasons Hotel now attracts golfing Americans.

Arriving in Nevis
Getting there The **Vance W Amory International Airport** is not large enough to receive long-haul flights so visitors from North America or Europe have to fly to St Kitts and get the ferry over, or to St Martin, Antigua or Puerto Rico and get a regional flight from there.

Getting around The main road around Nevis is only 20 miles, so it doesn't take long to circumnavigate this small island of 36 sq miles. There are taxis, rental cars, buses (minivans) and bicycle hire, or you can walk.

Charlestown
The main town is Charlestown, one of the best-preserved old towns in the Caribbean, with several interesting buildings dating from the 18th century. It is small and compact, on Gallows Bay, guarded by Fort Charles to the south and the long sweep of Pinney's Beach to the north. Nevis had the only court in the West Indies to try and hang pirates. Prisoners were taken from the courthouse across the swamp to where the gallows were set up, hence the name, Gallows Bay. There are plans for a national park to protect the swamp, which is a habitat for many birds, animals and plants.

    D R Walwyn's Plaza is dominated by the balconied **Old Customs/Treasury House**, built in 1837 and restored in 2002. The **tourist office** is here. **Memorial Square**, to the south, is larger and more impressive; the war memorial is in a small garden. The **Courthouse and Library** ⓘ *Mon-Fri 0900-1800, Sat 0900-*

1700 (the courthouse is closed to the public, except when a case is in progress), were built here in 1825 and used as the Nevis Government Headquarters, but were largely destroyed by fire in 1873 and subsequently rebuilt. The building still houses the library upstairs and the Nevis High Court and Registrar below. The little square tower was erected in 1909 to 1910. It contains a clock which keeps accurate time with an elaborate pulley and chain system. In the library you can see it, together with the weights, among the roof trusses.

Nevis

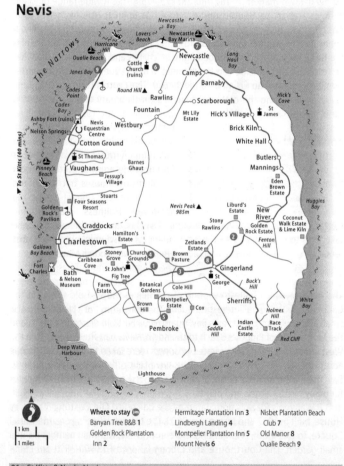

Where to stay	Hermitage Plantation Inn 3	Nisbet Plantation Beach
Banyan Tree B&B 1	Lindbergh Landing 4	Club 7
Golden Rock Plantation	Montpelier Plantation Inn 5	Old Manor 8
Inn 2	Mount Nevis 6	Oualie Beach 9

Along Government Road is the well-preserved **Jewish Cemetery**. The earliest evidence of a Jewish community on the island dates from 1677 to 1678, when there were four families. By the end of the century there were 17 households, a thriving synagogue and part of the main street was known as Jew Street, but invasion by the French in 1706 and 1783, hurricanes and the decline of the sugar industry in the 18th century led to an economic downturn and emigration. By the end of the 18th century only three Jewish households remained, and now there is no evidence of their presence except for the cemetery where 19 stones date from 1679-1730.

Charlestown **market** ① *Tue, Thu, Sat 0730-1500*, has a wide range of island produce and crafts. Housed under a roof but open to the elements, local farmers bring their produce to sell, with Saturday being the busiest day. It can be fascinating to wander around trying to identify fruits and vegetables and there is usually a good range of ginger, chillies and other spices. Stalls set up on the streets outside can be cheaper. Market Street to the right houses the **Philatelic Bureau** ① *Mon-Fri 0800-1600*. The **Cotton Ginnery** was, until 1994, in use during the cotton-picking season (February to July). In 1995 it was moved out to the New River Estate, Gingerland, where it is in a renovated building next to the sugar mill ruins there. As part of the Nevis Port upgrade, another Cotton Ginnery building now houses gift shops and a restaurant. On Chapel Street the **Wesleyan Holiness Manse**, built in 1812, is one of the oldest stone buildings surviving on the island, while the **Methodist Manse** (next to the prominent church) has the oldest wooden structure, the second floor was built in 1802.

The **Museum of Nevis History** ① *between Main St and the sea, T869-469 5786, www.nevis-nhcs.org, Mon-Fri 0900-1600, Sat 0900-1200, US$5*, at the Birthplace of Alexander Hamilton, is next to the sea and set in an attractive garden. The original house was built around 1680 but destroyed in the 1840s, probably by an earthquake. This house was rebuilt in 1983 on the foundations of the original structure

Charlestown

Where to stay 🛏
JP's 1

Restaurants 🍴
Café des Arts 1
Rivière House 2

and dedicated during the islands' Independence celebration in September of that year. The Nevis House of Assembly meets in the rooms upstairs, while the rather cramped museum occupies the ground floor. Alexander Hamilton, Nevis' most famous son, was born here on 11 January 1757. He lived on Nevis for only five years before leaving for St Croix with his family. About half of the display is given over to memorabilia and pictures of his life. The rest contains examples of Amerindian pottery, African culture imported by the slaves, cooking implements and recipes, a rum still, a model of a Nevis lighter, the ceremonial clothes of the Warden which were worn on the Queen's birthday and Remembrance Day and a section on nature conservation. A small shop sells local produce and some interesting books. All proceeds go to the upkeep of the museum.

Around the island

Taking the road south out of Charlestown, you can visit the rather unkempt **Fort Charles**. Fork right at the Shell station and again at the mini-roundabout, keep right along the sea shore (rough track), past the wine company and through gates at the end of the track. The fort was built before 1690 and altered many times before being completed 1783-1790. Not much remains apart from the circular well and a small building (possibly the magazine). The gun emplacements looking across to St Kitts are being badly eroded by the sea, some cannon have been moved to hotels. The Nevis Council surrendered to the French here in 1782 during the siege of Brimstone Hill on St Kitts.

Back on the main road and only about half a mile outside Charlestown lies the former **Bath Hotel** and **Spring House**. Built by the Huggins family in 1778, it is reputed to be one of the oldest hotels in the Caribbean and in its day hosted many illustrious figures as overnight guests or at its social functions. After a period of abandonment, the hotel has been restored and is in use as government offices. The Spring House lies over a fault which supplies constant hot water at 108°F, but is unusable unfortunately as the pipes supplying the water have become blocked. However, two thermal dipping pools have been constructed a bit further down stream, one of which has a roof to shade you from the sun. They are free for all to use and are very hot. Reputedly good for arthritis, immersion is not recommended for people with a heart condition and no one should stay in for more than 15 minutes. The water, being spring fed, is very clean.

The **Horatio Nelson Museum** ① *Belle Vue, next to Government House, T869-469 5786, www.nevis-nhcs.org/nelsonmuseum.html, Mon-Fri 0900-1600, Sat 0900-1200, US$5*, is based on a collection donated by Mr Robert Abrahams, an American who lived on the island. The museum contains Nelson memorabilia including letters, china, pictures, furniture and books (request to see the excellent collection of historical documents and display of 17th-century clay pipes) and a replica of Nelson's military uniform. Nelson was not always popular, having come to the island to enforce the Navigation Acts which forbade the newly independent American states trading with British colonies. In his ship *HMS Boreas,* he impounded four American ships and their cargoes. The Nevis merchants immediately claimed £40,000 losses against Nelson, who had to remain on board his ship for eight weeks to escape being put into gaol. It was only after Prince William, captain of *HMS Pegasus,* arrived in Antigua that Nelson gained social acceptability and married the widow, Fanny Woodward Nisbett (reputedly for her uncle's money; this proved a disappointment as her uncle left the island and spent his wealth in London). The museum also contains some pre-Columbian artefacts and displays on local history, including sugar and slavery. Outside, behind the museum rests the *Pioneer,* a Nevis lighter and the last sugar boat sailing to St Kitts. There are plans to renovate it, but to get a better idea of what it looked like, there is a model in the museum. There is also a gift shop.

More evidence of the Nelson connection is found at the **St John's Fig Tree Anglican Church** about two miles on from the Bath House. Originally built in 1680, the church was rebuilt in 1838 and again in 1895. The marriage certificate of Nelson and Fanny Nisbett is displayed here. There are interesting memorials to Fanny's father William Woodward and also to her first husband Dr Josiah Nisbett. Many died of fever during this period and if you lift the red carpet in the central aisles you can see old tombstones, many connected with the then leading family, the Herberts. The graveyard has many examples of tombstones in family groups dating from the 1780s. Nevis is divided into five parishes, each with its own Anglican church, but these make up a tiny fraction of the more than 80 churches for other denominations on the island. On Sunday church bells start ringing from 0600, calling the faithful to services lasting three hours or more, and it is a quiet day everywhere.

Slightly off the main road to the south lies **Montpelier Great House** where the marriage of Nelson and Mrs Nisbett actually took place; a plaque is set in the gatepost. The plantation is now a hotel with pleasant gardens; a great place for lunch or a drink. Enormous toads live in the lily ponds formed out of old sugar pans. Beyond the house lies **Saddle Hill** (1250 ft). It has the remains of a small fort, **Saddle Hill Battery**, and it is reputedly where Nelson would look out for illegal shipping. Nevisians had a grandstand view from here of the siege of Brimstone Hill by the French in 1782. You can follow several goat/nature trails on the hill; a track starts at Clay Ghaut, but most trails beyond the fort are dense and overgrown (giant aloes abound). Near Montpelier are the **Botanical Gardens** ① *T869-469 3509, www.botanicalgardennevis.com, gardens Mon-Sat 0900-1600, US$13, children US$8,* 7 acres of nicely laid out plants from around the world: cactus, bamboo, orchids, flowering trees and shrubs, heliconias and rose gardens, a mermaid fountain, a greenhouse with bridges, ponds, waterfall, bee hives for honey, a restaurant for lunch and a gift shop. The landscaping is beautiful and it is the perfect spot for relaxation, picnics, small gatherings and weddings, but it's not wheelchair friendly.

The small parish of **Gingerland** is reached after about three miles. Its rich soils made it the centre of the island's ginger root production (also cinnamon and nutmeg), but it is noteworthy for the very unusual octagonal Methodist church built in 1830. You turn right here along Hanleys Road to reach the excellent **White Bay Beach**. Go all the way down to the bottom and turn left at the Indian Castle experimental farm, past the race course (on Black Bay) and Red Cliff. There is a small shelter but no general shade. Beware, this is the Atlantic coast, the sea can be very rough and dangerous. On quieter days, the surf is fun and there are good views across to Montserrat. On the Atlantic side of Nevis the beaches tend to be rocky and the swimming treacherous. On the way back beware of the deep storm drain crossing the road near the church.

After Gingerland the land becomes more barren and this side of the island is much drier. Several sugar mills were built here because of the wind, notably **Coconut Walk Estate**, **New River Estate** (fairly intact) and the **Eden Brown Estate**, built around 1740. The latter was has the reputation of being haunted. A duel took place between the groom and the bride's brother at the wedding of Julia Huggins. The brother was killed and the fiancé fled the island to escape trial and execution. Heartbroken, Julia became a recluse and the Great House was abandoned. Although government-owned and open to the public, the ruins are in poor condition and care should be taken.

The island road continues north through Butlers and Brick Kiln (known locally as Brick Lyn), past St James' Church (Hick's village), Long Haul Bay and Newcastle Bay (with the **Nisbet Plantation Inn**) to the small fishing community of Newcastle and the airport. You can visit the **Newcastle Pottery** where distinctive red clay is used to make, among other things, the traditional Nevis cooking pot. The pottery is fired in the traditional manner over the hot embers of burned coconut husks.

The road continues through an increasingly fertile landscape, and there are fine views across the Narrows to the southeast peninsula of St Kitts, with **Booby Island** in the middle of the channel, the latter being mostly inhabited by pelicans (all birds are referred to as boobies by the local population). It offers good diving. The small hill on your left is **Round Hill** (1014 ft). It can be reached on the road between Cades Bay and Camps Village. Turn off the road at Fountain village by the Methodist church. There are good views from the radio station at the top over Charlestown, across to St Kitts and beyond to Antigua. There is a small beach at **Mosquito Bay** and some good snorkelling under the cliffs of Hurricane Hill. The **Oualie Beach Hotel** offers watersport facilities including scuba diving and snorkelling equipment. On Sunday afternoons there is often live music and a barbecue at Mosquito Bay. Sailing trips can be negotiated with locals.

Horse racing Nevis-style

The **Nevis Turf and Jockey Club** (www.facebook.com/ntajc) meets at least six times a year to race island thoroughbreds on the Indian Castle race course on Black Bay: New Year's Day, Tourism Week (February), Easter, May Day, August during Culturama, Independence Day and Boxing Day. Facilities include a grandstand seating 200, washrooms, a pari-mutuel booth, good food from vendors and dancing well into the night; this is part folk festival, part carnival, with no social barriers. There is a minimum of five races on the seaside track, from where you can see Redonda, Montserrat and Antigua in the distance and often whales spouting or breaching. The gates open at 1300, entrance US$7.50, children half price. Races start at 1500 and end at dusk. There is an average of four horses in each race, run clockwise over a distance of 5½ to 8 furlongs (one mile), with a hill up to the home stretch. Contact Richard Lupinacci, who resurrected racing in the 1980s, at the Hermitage Inn for details, T869-469 3477. You should also look out for the more amusing donkey races. Nevis is known for its large number of donkeys.

Under Round Hill on part of the 980-acre Round Hill Estate lies **Cottle Church** (1824). Built by John Cottle, a plantation owner, so that slaves could be taught and could worship with their masters, it was never consecrated as the practice was illegal at the time. It was also known as St Marks of Ease chapel. The chapel was severely damaged by the 1974 earthquake and Hurricane Hugo in 1989. Under restoration, its beautiful little font can be seen in the Museum of Nevis History (see page 97). Nearby, just off the island road, lies **Fort Ashby**, which protected Jamestown, the original settlement and former capital, which was supposedly destroyed by an earthquake and tidal wave in 1690, and was originally called St James's Fort. Fort Ashby is now in a very overgrown state with just some sections of wall remaining and some cannon. The outer wall used to be on the sea front but the shape of the coast has changed over the centuries and it is now inland. Near here is a freshwater lagoon fed by **Nelson's Spring**, which used to be a source of fresh water for sailing ships. Now it is worth seeing for its flowering water lilies, birds and butterflies. Drive past Nelson Spring (where the barrels from *HMS Boreas* were filled) and **St Thomas's Church** (built in 1643, one of the oldest surviving in the Caribbean) to the beautiful four-mile **Pinney's Beach**. There are many tracks leading down to the beach, often with a small hut or beach bar at the end of them. It is only a few minutes' walk from Charlestown and never crowded. The **Four Seasons Hotel** lies in the middle of the beach. The sunloungers are for guests only, but the public has access to the beach and there are watersports available. Behind the resort is the **Robert Trent Jones II** golf course which straddles the island road. The manicured fairways and greens are in marked contrast with the quiet beauty of the rest of the island but the hotel's considerable efforts at landscaping have lessened its impact.

◉ St Kitts and Nevis listings

For hotel and restaurant price codes and other relevant information, see pages 12-16.

⬛ Where to stay

St Kitts *p81, maps p82 and p84*
There is a 10% VAT and 10% service charge.
$$$$ Ocean Terrace Inn (OTI), Wigley Av, Basseterre, T869-465 2754, www.oceanterraceinn.com. Under renovation in 2014, to reopen as a modern, upmarket boutique hotel with rooms, suites and all mod cons. **Pro-Divers** and **Fisherman's Wharf** across the road on the water front.
$$$$ Ottley's Plantation Inn, Cayon, T869-465 7234, www.ottleys.com. 520 ft above sea level in 35 acres with views to the Atlantic. Rooms in the 1832 Great House or in luxury modern cottages in the beautiful tropical gardens with sweeping lawns and palm trees. Rooms are spacious and elegantly furnished, with large bathrooms, a/c, fans, plunge pools. The full-size pool is in the ruins of a sugar estate. Run by a US family who are very hospitable and knowledgeable. There are nice walks in the area or you can take the beach shuttle. Popular spa for massages in a little chattel house in the trees. The excellent **Royal**

Palm restaurant caters for all diets and provides elegant dining in a cool, natural environment built into the side of old sugar mill buildings.
$$$$ Rock Haven Bed & Breakfast, Scenic Drive, Frigate Bay, T869-465 5503, www.rock-haven.com. 2 suites at this B&B, with views of both coasts; one has a kitchen, patio, its own private entrance and can sleep 3, the other sleeps 2 and has a/c. Transport on arrival and departure included. Lovely views from the breakfast area upstairs where you are served a substantial and beautifully decorated breakfast with home-made bread. Genial hosts, a popular place with people who avoid hotels; book ahead.
$$$$-$$$ Timothy Beach Resort, 1 South Frigate Bay Beach, T869-465 8597, www.timothybeach.com. The only hotel in this area actually on the Caribbean. Good value, unpretentious, comfortable, accommodating staff. Various rooms and studios with kitchens, which can be connected to make apartments or a townhouse to sleep 2-10, mountain or sea view. Pool (where monkeys come to drink), steps down to the sea, Wi-Fi, **Sunset Café** for local food and burgers, good quality and value. Plenty of bars within walking distance for nightlife.

$$$ Mule House, Brighton Plantation, T869-466 8086, www.homeaway.co.uk. Brighton is the oldest plantation on the island and the **Mule House** has been built on the site of the former mule barn in the plantation yard. 4 self-catering apartments, each with their own entrance, kitchen, lounge/diner, Wi-Fi, huge shower room and 2 bedrooms with mosquito nets, books and a balcony with sea view. Fruit and flowers from the beautiful garden, Sue or Ray will meet you at the airport and help with excursions or car hire. Home from home, quiet and relaxing.

$$$ Seaview Inn, Bay Rd, Basseterre, T869-466 1635, http://seaviewinn.cbt.cc. There is no sea view, but if you want to stay in Basseterre, this is a reasonable option, good value, simply furnished, clean, with a bar, restaurant and attentive service.

$$$-$$ Fern Tree Bed & Breakfast, Paradise Rd, Conaree, T869-466 9843, http://stkitts-bed-breakfast.com. Charming hosts and a substantial breakfast make this one of the best-value places to stay if you don't mind being away from the beach. 5 mins from the airport and 100 yds from a bus stop, sea views on one side and mountain views on the other.

Nevis *p95, maps p96 and p97*
A 10% VAT plus 2% Nevis tourism promotion tax and 10% service charge are levied.

$$$$ Banyan Tree Bed & Breakfast, T869-469 3449, www.banyantreebandb.com. 15 Nov-15 Apr. 2 charming rooms in the guesthouse and 1-bedroom suite with kitchenette in **Bamboo House**, all with verandas, 700 ft above sea level near Morning Star village on a 6-acre farm growing flowers, spices (try the ginger tea) and raising Barbados black-belly sheep, lots of fruit trees and a 300-year-old banyan tree.

$$$$ Golden Rock Plantation Inn, St George's Parish, T869-469 3346, http://goldenrocknevis.com. This 100-acre 18th-century plantation house on a hillside is a peaceful, private oasis. 11 charming rooms in cottages, are simple but comfortable in wonderful gardens with fish ponds. There's also a 2-storey suite in the old windmill for honeymooners/families, with antique furniture and 4-poster beds. Plenty of breeze up on the hill, no a/c needed, ocean view all the way to Montserrat, pool (formerly the sugar mill cistern), bike rental, excellent hiking, enjoy afternoon tea and watch the monkeys.

$$$$ Hermitage Plantation Inn, St John's Parish, T869-469 3477, www.hermitagenevis.com. Beautiful wooden cottages, all different, some rather small, 4-poster beds. The **Planter's House** dates from 1680-1740 and is believed to be the oldest wooden house in the Lesser Antilles, old furniture and prints on the walls, chintz furnishings, tennis, pool, stunning rural setting with views down to the sea, equestrian/adventure/diving packages offered, stables on site. Lunch on the terrace, dinner indoors, lamb and pork are home-grown, as are the fruit and vegetables. They also have their own boat, rigged for fishing, which is used to ferry guests from St Kitts, as well as for snorkelling trips and sunset sails.

$$$$ Montpelier Plantation Inn and Beach Club, T869-469 3462, www.montpeliernevis.com. The Hoffman family run this beautiful old property on 30 acres, 750 ft above sea level. You are welcomed with cold towels and rum punch. Delightful, friendly and helpful, long-serving staff, pool, tennis, lovely gardens, beach shuttle, discounts for children, rooms painted white with cool green or blue flourishes, fresh fruit daily. 3 restaurants (including a small, intimate one inside the old mill), all of which offer gourmet food from local or home-grown ingredients, whether it's a light lunch or sumptuous multi-course tasting menu for dinner accompanied by fine wines and followed by fine aged rums.

$$$$ Mount Nevis, Shaws Rd, Newcastle, T869-469 9373, www. mountnevishotel.com. Not a plantation inn and not on the beach, but this hotel on 17 acres on a hillside overlooking St Kitts is well regarded. Comfortable, with excellent service, a good pool and pleasant, open air restaurant, it is quiet and peaceful.

$$$$ Nisbet Plantation Beach Club, St James, on a ½-mile beach close to the airport, T869-469 9325, www.nisbetplantation.com. The only plantation inn on the beach, 36 comfortable rooms in hexagonal cottages/suites in the gardens of the 1776 Great House, spread out down the hill to the sea, a/c, fans, tennis, pool, croquet, beach bar for lunch, restaurant, bar and TV lounge, huge

breakfasts, delicious afternoon tea and great dinner included.

$$$$ The Old Manor, T869-469 3445, www.oldmanornevis.com. This restored 1690 sugar plantation has 12 spacious rooms and suites which incorporate the stone walls of the old mill buildings, with wooden walls, shutters and louvred windows, each with veranda, fridge, coffee maker, etc. 800 ft above sea level, delightfully breezy and cool, no a/c needed, old furnishings, and prints of old maps on the walls, good restaurant with views to Montserrat, tropical gardens, beach shuttle, pool, spa services.

$$$$ Oualie Beach Hotel, T869-469 9735, www.oualiebeach.com. Comfortable, well-equipped rooms/ studios, in cottages with views over the bay, deluxe rooms on the beach, a/c, fans, TV, non-smoking, massage room, meal plans and other packages available. Relaxed bar and restaurant on the sand under tamarind trees: surf-and-turf beach barbecue on Tue with rhythm and blues, manager's cocktail party Wed with live music, booze cruise Thu in season, Fri happy hour with live bands. Mountain bikes, diving, kayaking and other watersports.

$$$$-$$$ Lindbergh Landing, Dr Penn Heights, Church Ground, T869-469 3398, http://lindbergh landingnevis.com. Sweet little wooden cottages high on the hillside with views down to the coast, with kitchenettes, although breakfast is available, family-run, knowledgeable hosts. Bar and food service some lunchtimes/evenings, nature walks offered on trails from the property.

$$$ JP's, Lower Prince William St, in town near pier and market, T869-469 0319. Popular with yachties wanting terra firma or anyone on a budget, simple rooms, a/c, fans, fridge, Wi-Fi, lounge with TV, restaurant. No staff on premises at night or on Sun.

❼ Restaurants

St Kitts *p81, maps p82 and p84*
Restaurants usually add 10% service, 10% VAT and 2% ISF tax.

$$$ Circus Grill, The Circus, Basseterre, T869-465 0143, see Facebook. Mon-Sat 1100-2100. Good well-presented food and friendly staff. More expensive and formal than **Ballahoo** but popular with the office trade as well as visitors. Variety of menu options including Asian fusion.

$$$ Lion Rock Beach Bar, Cockleshell Bay, T869-663 8711, https://lion rockbeachbar.shutterfly.com. Unprepossessing shack on the beach run by Lion and Angela to great acclaim. Go for a relaxing day on the beach with a sunbed (2 chairs and shade US$10), an ice-cold beer or killer rum punch, maybe a massage and eat chicken, ribs or fish with coconut rice. Call ahead or come early for lunch as they close the kitchen if there aren't many guests.

$$$ Marshall's, at **Horizons Villa Resort**, Frigate Bay, T869-466 8245. Daily 1800-2200. Romantic poolside dining with an ocean view, great sunsets, exquisite food, not to be missed. Visitors come here for fine dining and locals use it for special occasions.

$$$ PJ's, Frigate Bay North, T869-465 8373. Close to the **Marriott** and popular as an escape to eat pizza. Good company too, with the bar propped up by a regular local clientele.

$$$ Reggae Beach Bar and Grill, Cockleshell Bay, T869-762 5050, www.reggaebeachbar.com. Daily 1000-1700 for lunch, lobster-fest dinner Fri night. Good food, mostly fish, shrimp, conch and lobster but also chicken, burgers and vegetarian options. Lots of fun, popular, good cocktails. Snorkelling gear, beach chairs and kayaks for hire.

$$$ Rituals Sushi, Frigate Bay North, overlooking the golf course, T869-466 0161. If you fancy something a bit different, this is an authentic sushi restaurant with a good selection of Japanese dishes. Eat indoors with the Japanese decor or outside on the patio.

$$$ Rock Lobster, St Christopher Club, Frigate Bay, T869-466 1092. Bar from 1500, restaurant from 1700. The name speaks for itself – the lobster rocks! Also fish, seafood platter, tapas, steak, nachos, à la carte, full bar. There is inside and outside seating. Located close to the sea shore in the resort area. Great weekend spot, closes when the action stops.

$$$-$$ Bombay Blues, Frigate Bay North. If you crave an authentic Indian curry, this is the place to come, with good use of seasonings in all the usual offerings, tandoori, naans, plenty of vegetarian dishes and an excellent Sun brunch buffet.

$$$-$$ Buddies Beach Hut, The Strip, South Frigate Bay, T869-465 2839. Mon-Fri from 1700, Sat, Sun from 1100. Stays open at weekends until the last guest leaves. Good-value cook-up, spare ribs, fries, garlic bread, on the beach, no need to pack a picnic basket. Bar downstairs, dance floor upstairs.

$$$-$$ El Fredo's, Bay Rd on the corner with Sandown, Basseterre, T869-466 8871. A good local lunch spot, serving typical dishes such as goat water, oxtail, pigtail soup and steamed fresh fish served with plantain and other traditional accompaniments.

$$$-$$ Jam Rock Beach Bar, South Friars Bay, T869-469 1608. Jamaican-owned so expect jerk chicken and pork on the menu, but there is also some good fish and the grouper is excellent.

$$$-$$ Serendipity Restaurant and Lounge Bar, 3 Wigley Av, Fortlands, T869-465 9999, http:// serendipitystkitts.com. Lunch Tue-Fri 1130-1500, dinner Tue-Sun 1800-2200, may close early if not busy, closed public holidays, reservations essential. Premier fine dining experience overlooking the Basseterre coastline from the veranda, excellent service and meals with Caribbean and European dishes.

$$$-$$ Shiggedy Shack, The Strip, South Frigate Bay, T869-465 0673. The opposite end of the row of bars from Buddies. Sit at wooden benches and tables on the sand, grilled fresh fish, lobster and other seafood, popular fish burgers. Also live entertainment and karaoke nights.

$$$-$$ Star of India, Victoria Rd, Basseterre, T869-466 1537. Mon-Sat 0900-2200. Chef from Mumbai, authentic Indian food with good tandoori and curries. Many locals get takeaway; there is seating but it's not very private. Good Wed buffet. Student discounts and delivery available.

$$$-$$ Sunset Beach Bar, South Friars Bay. Now moved along the beach from its original location to make way for the Carambola, this long-established beach bar serves local food such as stew chicken or steamed fish, served with peas and rice. Friendly and welcoming.

$$$-$$ Sweet Cane, Port Zante, Basseterre, T869-665 7628. Eclectic menu, something for everyone, from pasta to grouper, jerk chicken to beef in red wine sauce. Good service, well-cooked food and convenient location in the cruise ship complex.

$$ Sprat Net, Old Road Town, by the sea, T869-466 7535. Thu-Sun. Run by the Spencer family, this is one of the places to be at weekends, when it gets busy. People come from all over the island for their fresh fish and goat water. Highly recommended for a good atmosphere and reasonably priced food. Watch your fish being cooked on an open grill and eat at wooden picnic tables.

$$-$ Ballahoo, corner of Bank St and Fort St, Basseterre, T869-465 4197, www.ballahoo.com. Mon-Sat 0800-2200. Great central meeting place with a fun, laid-back atmosphere, lovely view of The Circus, excellent local food at reasonable prices. A favourite with visitors who like to sit overlooking the bustle of the town centre from the terrace on the first floor.

Nevis *p95, maps p96 and p97*
In restaurants VAT of 10% plus 2% (Nevis tourism promotion tax) is charged to your bill and a 10-15% tip is expected or added.

$$$ Bananas, Upper Hamilton Estate, T869-469 1891, www. bananasrestaurantnevis.com. Mon-Sat 1230-1530, 1800-2200, reservations recommended for dinner. Set in a lush garden, the restaurant is in an attractive wooden house with a wraparound veranda, very romantic at night. Inside, the walls are covered with regional art work. British chef, former dancer, Gillian Smith, serves up delicious meals including lobster in season and Moroccan-style lamb shanks, a wonderful mix of local specialities, together with Asian, Mediterranean and veggie options. Service is most hospitable.

$$$ Coconut Grove, Main Island Rd, Clifton Estate, T869-469 1020, www. coconutgroverestaurantnevis.com. Lunch and dinner. Gourmet restaurant on the beach, French cuisine and local seafood are a wonderful marriage. Varied wine list from around the world. High end with prices to match but a great place for a special meal. Open air under thatched roof.

$$$ Double Deuce Restaurant and Bar, Pinney's Beach, T869-469 2222, www.doubledeucenevis.com. Tue-Sun 0900-until the last customer leaves. Specializes in local sea foods such as *mahi mahi*, lobster, snapper, conch as well as really good burgers. **The Bar** is also open on Thu for karaoke from 2100 until late. Fri mussels, burgers, Sat dance night from 2200, Sun is

roast beef and Yorkshire pudding, while in the afternoon there is bingo. There is also table tennis, pool tables, darts board, a swimming pool, Wi-Fi and book exchange library.

$$$ Lime Beach Bar, Pinney's Beach, T869-469 1147. Lunch and dinner Mon-Sat, live band Fri night. Set back a bit off the beach, Lime offers simple but good fare off the grill, including burgers, fish, chicken and lobster.

$$$ The Rocks, Golden Rock Plantation Inn, T869-469 3346, http:// goldenrocknevis.com. Delightful location overlooking Montserrat surrounded by beautiful gardens. There are several tables dotted around in private spots away from the main restaurant area. Very good food, a nice place to stop for lunch, even just for a sandwich, but the full meals are excellent, emphasizing local ingredients to go with the catch of the day. Lobster in season always well prepared. Good wine list too.

$$$ Sunshine Beach Bar & Grill, Pinney's Beach, www.sunshinesnevis. com. Daily with lunch 1200-1530, dinner 1800-2130, bar has longer hours. Casual beach bar, colourful and laid back with friendly staff. Salads, burgers, wings, ribs, lobster sandwich or food from the grill: fish, chicken, lobster, shrimp. The signature cocktail is a 'killer bee': rum with passion fruit.

$$$ Yachtsman Grill, on the beach in front of the Hamilton Beach Villas and close to **Funky Monkey** tours, T869-469 1382, http://yachtsmangrill. com. Lunch and dinner daily. Fri evening live music. Modern, smart beach restaurant and bar serving good quality, fresh food, more upmarket than most other beach bars, with items such as seared tuna on the menu as well as lobster. You can also get a great thin crust pizza here, cooked in a wood-fired oven and made with flour and other ingredients imported from Naples.

$$$-$$ Café des Arts, between the museum and the waterfront, Charlestown, T869-667 8768. Mon-Sat breakfast, lunch and dinner. Good for salads, sandwiches, quiche, tables outside under the trees and parasols. Tue night burger night, including veggie burgers.

$$$-$$ Oasis in the Gardens, Botanical Gardens, Montpelier Estate, T869-469 2875, www.botanicalgarden nevis.com. Mon-Sat 1000-1700, only open for dinner Mon and Fri and for tapas Sat afternoon. In the upper part of the Great House, serving Thai food. A popular lunch spot or for a drink during a tour of the gardens.

$$$-$$ Rivière House, Government Rd, Charleston, T869-469 7117, www. rivierehouseandcottagesnevis.com. Breakfast and lunch Mon-Sat, dinner Thu-Sat. Pleasant plantation-style building serving good-value food, local and international dishes, a pizza menu, plenty of parking and Wi-Fi.

🎷 Bars and clubs

St Kitts *p81, maps p82 and p84*
South Frigate Bay is lined with bars, restaurants and rum shacks, familiarly known as 'The Strip'. You can wander along the beach doing a 'pub crawl', choosing the atmosphere that suits you. Some have live music some nights or a DJ, or there might be volleyball matches and other entertainment, such as the fire show at **Mr X's Shiggidy Shack** on Thu night. **Patsy's** has a live band on Sun and karaoke on Wed. **Vibes** hosts 'Finally Friday' with DJ on Fri and 'Surprise Saturday' with live band on Sat (open until 0300) and is more of a sports bar/nightclub than some others.

Green Valley Pub, Main St, Cayon, T869-465 3104. Mon-Sat 1000-2400. With 2 levels, you can sit with your rum or beer upstairs overlooking the stage below. Live music and dances are held regularly. The **Green Valley Festival** in May is one of the best community events on St Kitts, a mini-Carnival when the whole area comes alive for calypso and parades.

Karma Lounge & Bar, Sugars Complex, Frigate Bay, T869-762 5501, see Facebook. Daily 1700-0100. Widescreen TVs and music with Asian restaurant alongside. There is a huge selection of beers from over 40 different countries. Guest international DJs once a month.

Royal Beach Casino, at the **St Kitts Marriott Resort**, Frigate Bay, T869-466 5555, www.royalbeachcasino.net. Gaming tables (from 1600, depending on demand and season), slot machines (Mon-Thu 1200-0200, Fri 1200-0400, Sat 1000-0400, Sun 1000-0200) and kiosks for betting on sports, this is a glitzy Vegas-style, 35,000-sq-ft casino, offering free drinks for gamblers.

Rum Barrel, Port Zante, Basseterre, T869-760 8888. Mon-Sat 0800-2300. Great place for people-watching as this open-air bar is close to where the cruise ship passengers disembark. Friday after-work place for Kittitians when there is often a DJ raising the decibel level.

Twist Bar, Port Zante, Basseterre. Daily 1030-2100. Upstairs sports bar with flatscreen TVs showing major sporting events, plus a pool table and table football for entertainment. Food is available but the bar is known for its many Caribbean rums and cocktails.

Nevis *p95, maps p96 and p97*
Look for posters, radio announcements or ask what's on at the tourist office or one of the beach bars. The hotels usually have live music one night a week in season, although things get quieter in the summer. The beach bars along Pinney's Beach and some restaurants also offer live bands or a DJ or karaoke 1 or more nights a week.

○ Shopping

St Kitts *p81, maps p82 and p84*
Pelical Mall and **TDC Mall** have a range of shops selling clothing and souvenirs. The area around the cruise ship dock, Port Zante, is busy with boutiques and vendors. Local sea island cotton wear and cane and basketwork are attractive and reasonable. There are vendors' markets at the **Craft House** on the Bay Rd and on Lower College St Ghaut and Liverpool Row. Go to **Caribelle Batik**, at Romney Manor (see page 89), for a huge range of batik clothing and to see the way it is made.

Food
The public market in Basseterre is busiest Sat morning, good for fruit and vegetables, also fish stalls and butchers. Supermarkets in Basseterre include **B & K Superfood** on the south side of Independence Sq and George St, **Horsfords Valumart** on Wellington Rd, and **Rams** on Bay Rd, T869-466 7777, Frigate Bay and at Bird Rock.

Stamps
The St Kitts' philatelic bureau is in **Pelican Shopping Mall**, Mon-Wed, Fri-Sat 0800-1200, 1300-1500, Thu 0800-1100.

Nevis *p95, maps p96 and p97*
Art galleries
Eva Wilkin Gallery, Clay Ghaut, Gingerland, T869-469 2673. Mon-Fri 1000-1500. Started by Howard and Marlene Paine, it has an exhibition in an 18th-century windmill of paintings and drawings by Nevisian Eva Wilkin MBE (whose studio it was until her death in 1989), prints of which are available. Next to the windmill is a shop selling antique furniture, maps and other bits and pieces.

Crafts
Nevis Handicraft Co-operative, Main St, Charlestown, next to the tourist office, T869-469 1746. A good collection of local artisans' work. **Newcastle Pottery**, Newcastle. Mon-Fri 0900-1600. The pottery makes red clay artefacts including bowls and candleholders. You can watch potters at work. The kilns are fired by burning coconut husks.

Food

Supermarkets include **Nisbets** in Newcastle, **Rams** at Stoney Grove and **Superfood**, Parkville Plaza, Charlestown.

The public market in Charlestown is busiest Sat morning, good for fruit and vegetables, also fish stalls and butchers.

Stamps

Nevis Philatelic Bureau, Charlestown, Mon-Fri 0800-1600. Nevis is famous for its first-day covers of the island's fauna and flora, undersea life, history and carnival.

○ What to do

St Kitts *p81, maps p82 and p84*
Cricket

St Kitts and Nevis are cricket-mad and have produced 7 players, all from Nevis, to play in the West Indies team in Test matches. In Jul 2004 the sister islands were delighted to be picked to host matches in the 2007 Cricket World Cup. **Warner Park** outside Basseterre was built with financial assistance from Taiwan and all the jobs went to local people (unlike other grounds built with Chinese help and Chinese labour). The new stadium has a permanent capacity of 8000, although this was temporarily increased for the World Cup. It is small but scenic and well-designed, with the comfort in mind of players, media, officials and spectators.

Diving

There is very good snorkelling and scuba diving around St Kitts. Most dive sites are on the Caribbean side, where the reef starts in shallow water and falls off to 100 ft or more. Between the 2 islands there is a shelf in only 25 ft of water which attracts lots of fish, including angelfish, to the corals, sea fans and sponges. There is black coral off the southeast peninsula, coral caves, reefs and wrecks with abundant fish and other sea creatures of all sizes and colours. Off St Kitts good reefs to dive include **Turtle Reef** (off Shitten Bay) which is good for beginners and snorkelling, **Coconut Reef** in Basseterre Bay and **Pump Bay** by Sandy Point. Much of the diving is suitable for novices and few of the major sites are deeper than 70 ft.

Several wrecks and some other sites are actually shallow enough for very rewarding snorkelling although the very best snorkelling around St Kitts is only accessible by boat.

Dive St Kitts, South Pelican Drive, T869-465 8914, www.divestkitts.com. Fast, covered dive boat, friendly and helpful staff, PADI dive courses, individual dives with or without equipment hire and dive excursions for cruise ship passengers. Will match or beat competitors' prices.

Kenneth's Dive Centre, Bay Rd, Basseterre, T869-465 2670, http://kennethdivecenter.com. Kenneth Samuel runs the longest-established dive centre on St Kitts, with courses and dive packages (single-tank dive US$70 with your own equipment, US$80 including equipment, 2-tank dive US$105/115, 4-day package US$320/340). There are facilities for people with disabilities.

Pro-Divers St Kitts at Fisherman's Wharf, Basseterre, T869-660 3483, www.prodiverstkitts.com. A PADI 5-star dive centre. Large boat takes large parties diving, PADI instruction. Dive gear available for rent, dive packages available, single-tank dive US$70 with your own equipment, US$80 including equipment, 2-tank dive US$95/110, 4-day package US$320/380, half-day snorkelling US$50. Ocean kayaks for hire.

Fishing

Speedy 4 Charters, Frigate Bay, T869-662 3453, www.speedy4 charters.com. Capt Glen Guishard offers fishing and snorkelling trips including excursions to Nevis.
VIP Charters, Basseterre, T869-762 5410, www.vipcharters.net. Fishing charters, snorkelling trips and island-hopping excursions as far afield as St Barts.

Golf

Royal St Kitts Golf Club, Frigate Bay, T869-466 2700, www.royalstkittsgolf club.com. An 18-hole international championship golf course. Built on 125 acres, with 2 holes on the Caribbean and 3 holes on the Atlantic. Brackish water is used to irrigate the special grass which can tolerate salt. Green fees are US$165 for 18 holes, US$95 for 9 holes after 1300, reduced rate for hotel guests, juniors and discounts in summer.

Hiking

Greg's Safaris, T869-465 4121, www.gregsafaris.com. Pleasant and informative, US$40-80. 4 tours offered,

popular with cruise ship passengers so often large groups and not all involving hiking: full-day Mt Liamuiga volcano crater hike (US$105); half-day rainforest hike and Caribelle Batik factory tour (US$65); Phillips rainforest hike and 4WD safari (US$65); 4WD safari and beach time at Timothy Beach Resort, Frigate Bay (US$65); and 4WD plantation tour (US$65).

Horse racing

The **Beaumont Park Race Track,** Caines Estate, between Parsons Ground and Dieppe Bay, T869-465 1627. Opened in 2009 with a US$17 million investment, the track is open to horse racing and greyhound racing. The area is part of an exclusive but controversial development of homes on former sugar cane land.

Sailing

Blue Water Safaris, St Kitts, T869-466 4933, www.bluewatersafaris.com. 4 catamarans take 12-90 passengers on a variety of cruises from whole day to sunset cruises. Kayak tours of the southeast peninsula (US$50) also available.
Leeward Island Charters, Fort St, Basseterre, St Kitts, T869-465 7474. *Caona II*, a 47-ft catamaran based in Nevis, 67-ft *Eagle*, or *Spirit of St Kitts*, a 70-ft catamaran for a sail to Nevis, snorkel and barbecue on a beach.

Tour operators

Caribbean Journey Masters, Island Paradise Commercial Complex, Frigate Bay, T869-466 8110, www. caribbeanjourneymasters.com.

Party bus, pub crawls and charters. For those who like riotous entertainment, friendly tour guides takes you on a crazy tour bus with lots of music – unforgettable. Full range of tours offered, from volcano hike to catamaran tours.

Nevis *p95, maps p96 and p97*
Cycling
Bike, Kayak 'n' Windsurf' Nevis, beside the Oualie Beach Club, T869-664 2843, www.bikenevis.com. Includes the **Wheel World Cycle Shop**, T869-469 9682. Winston Crooke organizes bike tours, hike'n'bike tours, and early morning bike rides. Bikes for hire, US$25-35 a day, include mountain bikes, road bikes, hybrid bikes, tandems, BMX, junior MRB and other fun bikes for kids, while for smaller children there are child seats or tandem attachments. There are often competitions going on. Winston is president of the St Kitts & Nevis Triathlon Federation, General Secretary of the Cycling Federation, event organizer for the annual Nevis Triathlon, the Nevis to St Kitts Cross Channel Swim and the Nevis Half Marathon running race. Visitors are welcome to join in any training sessions.
Nevis Adventure Tours/Green Edge Bike Shop, Yamseed Rd, Newcastle Village, T869-765 4158, www.nevis adventuretours.com. Open 0830-1800. Bike rental US$30 a day, US$180 a week. Owned and run by Reggie Douglas, another fitness fanatic who has many times been the National Triathlon Champion, OECS Champion and St Kitts and Nevis Sportsman of the Year.

Diving
Scuba Safaris, Oualie Beach, T869-469 9518, www.divestkittsnevis. com. A 5-star operation run by Ellis Chaderton. 3 days of 2-tank dives costs US$300 plus US$20 a day for BCD/regulator rental, PADI instruction and equipment rental, PADI Open Water qualification US$550. Also trips to see dolphins and humpback whales Jan-Apr, and snorkelling tours.

Fishing
Nevis Fishing, Oualie Beach, T869-663 3301, www.nevisfishing.net. Clivin Christmas, captain of the *Blackfin* offers deep-sea fishing, reef fishing with light tackle, water taxi services or leisure tours. Oct-Dec is peak wahoo season, Feb-Apr is best for tuna and wahoo, Jun-Aug for billfish, all of which are released.

Golf
The Four Seasons, T869-469 1111. An excellent 18-hole, par 71 championship course designed by Robert Trent Jones Jr. People fly in from other islands just to play here. It is beautifully maintained and offers fabulous views, but green fees are US$160-235 depending on the time of year, with discounts for hotel guests.

For something completely different, the **Cat Ghaut Chip 'n' Putt Course** opposite the entrance to the **Mount Nevis Hotel**, T869-469 9826, is a 9-hole course over 14 acres, US$10, with a nature trail among fruit trees and plenty of fauna and flora.

Nevis diving

Snorkelling is excellent off **Oualie Beach** and is also good at **Nisbet Beach** and **Tamarind Bay**. Good dive sites include **Monkey Shoal**, where you can find angel fish, black durgons, octopus, flying gurnard and maybe nurse sharks in the overhangs, crevices and grottos of this densely covered reef. **Devil's Caves** are another series of grottos, where you can see lobster and squirrelfish and often turtles riding the surge. **Nag's Head**, just off Oualie Beach, is a schooling ground for big fish such as king mackerel, barracuda, jacks and yellowtail snappers. Some dive operators will take you as far as Redonda, where diving is superb and untouched.

Hiking

Nevis Adventure Tours, Yamseed Rd, Newcastle Village, T869-765 4158, www.nevisadventuretours.com. Reggie Douglas leads hikes up the 3232-ft volcano, 4-5 hrs up and down from the village of Zetlands, or a bit longer if you go up and over, finishing in Hamilton Estate. These hikes involve some scrambling and climbing, you should expect to get wet and muddy (see Facebook photos) and you must wear decent hiking boots. This is generally considered harder than the ascent of Mt Liamuiga on St Kitts, but it's extremely rewarding with fabulous views. There is also a hike through the rainforest on the Atlantic side of the island, starting at the old Russell Plantation ruins and passing waterfalls, with lots of plants and wildlife to see. Reggie is an attentive, helpful and informative guide.

Sunrise Tours, Gingerland, T869-469 2758. Trips to Nevis Peak (4-hr round trip, US$40), Saddle Hill (1½ hrs, US$30) or the Source Trail and Rainforest Hike (3 hrs, US$35) among others. Run by Lynnell Liburd and his son, Kervin.

Horse riding

Nevis horses are thoroughbred/Créole crosses, mostly retired from racing on Nevis, where it is the 2nd most popular sport after cricket.

Nevis is known for its large number of donkeys. A donkey ride is an unusual and exciting way to see the sights. Make sure you're wearing jeans. Some donkey rides are organized through hotels and tour agents.

Hermitage Plantation, T869-469 3477. Horse-drawn carriage tours and horse riding.

Nevis Equestrian Centre, Main Rd, Clifton Estate, Cotton Ground, T869-662 9118, www.nevishorseback.com. Run by John and Ali Jordan Guilbert and Erika Guilbert-Walters. 10 different rides from US$55 with a combination of trail and beach, English or Western saddles, for novice or experienced riders. There's also an arena for lessons,

US$30 per hr. They even have a 6-hr cross island ride, but don't try that if you're not used to sitting in a saddle.

Horse racing
The **Nevis Turf and Jockey Club** meets at least 6 times a year to race island thoroughbreds: New Year's Day, Tourism Week (Feb), Easter, May Day, Aug during Culturama, Independence Day and Boxing Day. Facilities past Market Shop and down Hanley's Rd include a grandstand seating 200, washrooms, a pari-mutuel booth, good food and dancing well into the night; this is part folk festival, part carnival, with no social barriers. There is a minimum of 5 races on the seaside track, where you can see Redonda, Montserrat and Antigua in the distance and often whales breaching. Races start mid-afternoon and end at dusk. An average of 4 horses in each race run clockwise over a distance of 5½ to 8 furlongs (1 mile), with a hill up to the home stretch. Contact Richard Lupinacci, who resurrected racing in the 1980s, at the **Hermitage Inn** for details, T860-469 3477. Look out for the more amusing donkey races.

Watersports
Bike, Kayak 'n' Windsurf' Nevis, beside the Oualie Beach Club, T869-664 2843, www.bikenevis.com. Windsurfing, rentals and lessons for all levels. Sea kayaks for hire, and tours along the coast with picnic are offered.

⊖ Transport

St Kitts *p81, maps p82 and p84*
Air
RL Bradshaw International Airport is 2 miles from Basseterre. There are taxis, which charge fixed rates for 1-4 passengers. Alternatively, when returning you can get a bus from the bus stop at the roundabout northeast of Independence Sq to the airport and walk the last 5 mins from the main road; some buses might go up to the terminal. If you don't have much luggage, it is easy to walk from Basseterre to the airport. There are duty-free and gift shops and a café, but they tend to open for long-haul flights only. Even the bar in the departure lounge is often shut.

Boat
Port Zante can accommodate 2 of the largest cruise ships. For ferry information to Nevis, see below.

Bus
Minibuses do not run on a scheduled basis, but follow a set route (more or less), EC$2.50-4 on most routes, frequent service from the bus terminal close to the market area on the Bay Rd from where buses go west to Sandy Point. Passengers pay upon entrance to the bus. To catch a bus east, wait off Bakers Corner at the east end of Cayon St. There are no minibuses to Frigate Bay and the southeast peninsula.

Car hire
If visiting at carnival time you should book car hire a long time in advance.

Companies insist on you having collision damage waiver, which adds another US$5-10 to quoted rates. There is also VAT on car rentals. Most rental companies will help you obtain the obligatory temporary driving licence, US$24 for 3 months, or US$45 valid for a year, from the Traffic Department or your rental company. If you rent for 3 days or more you can arrange for a car on the sister island and do a day trip to St Kitts or Nevis. For a list of hire companies, see the St Kitts tourist office website, http://www.stkittstourism.kn/explore-st-kitts-getting-around-car-rental.php.

Taxi
Taxis have a yellow T registration plate. There are taxi ranks at the Circus in Basseterre, Pelican Mall, the airport and at Frigate Bay, or your hotel can call one for you. Maximum taxi fares are fixed, for example from airport to Basseterre US$10-12, to Frigate Bay, US$16, to Sandy Point US$24. From Frigate Bay to Cockleshell Bay or Majors Bay is US$22. Round trip from Basseterre to Romney Manor US$40, to Brimstone Hill US$50. A southeast peninsula tour is US$52, an island tour excluding the southeast peninsula US$80. A 7-hr personalized tour with excursions to wherever you please costs US$250 for up to 4 people. A 50% extra charge is made on both islands between 2200 and 0600.

Nevis *p95, maps p96 and p97*
Air
Vance Amory International Airport is at Newcastle, 7 miles from Charlestown (on the main road, bus to Charlestown US$1.65). The terminal is new and smart and there is a Visa ATM. Expect to have your baggage searched on your way in.

Boat
The crossing between St Kitts and Nevis takes 45-60 mins and costs US$10 one way plus EC$1 tax (*Sea Hustler*, T869-469 0403; *Caribe Breeze* and *Caribe Surf*, T869-466 6734; *Mark Twain*, T869-469 0403). Several daily departures from 0700, depending on the boat. The *Seabridge* car ferry, T869-765 7053, links Major's Bay in the south of St Kitts with Cades Point on Nevis, running every 2 hrs during daylight hours, EC$75 for 1 car and a driver and EC$15 for each additional passenger. For sailing times, see http://www.thestkittsnevisobserver.com/ferry-schedules.html. Tickets can only be purchased from the quay just prior to departure, so turn up about 1 hr in advance.

The **Four Seasons Hotel** has ferry boats running exclusively for guests' flights. **Oualie Beach** also arranges transfers for guests from St Kitts Airport via Turtle Beach (day) or Port Zante (night) with a water taxi.

Water taxi Island tours operate from St Kitts and there is also a water taxi service between the 2 islands: US$25 return, minimum 4 passengers, 20 mins, operated by **Kenneth's Dive Centre**, or **Pro-Divers**, see under Diving, above.

Bus
Minibuses start outside **Foodworld Cash & Carry** and go to all points,

but are not very regular, EC$2.50-4; an island tour is possible, if time consuming. Buses have green licence plates starting with the letter H or HA. They run around the island main road and can be flagged down anywhere.

Car hire
Rental cars are easily distinguished by their red licence plates beginning with R or RA.

Taxi
Taxis have a yellow T registration plate. Maximum taxi fares are set, for example: a taxi from the airport to Charlestown costs US$15, to Oualie Beach, US$10. A 50% extra charge is made between 2200 and 0600. Tours of Nevis cost US$20 per hr and a whole-island tour costs US$60.

❶ Directory

St Kitts *p81, maps p82 and p84*
Medical services Joseph N France General Hospital, Cayon St, Basseterre, T869-465 2551, has a 24-hr A&E. There is no hyperbaric chamber; any diver requiring treatment is air-lifted to Saba. Most doctors and hospitals will expect payment in cash, regardless of whether you have health insurance.

Nevis *p95, maps p96 and p97*
Medical services The **Alexandra Hospital** is on Government Rd, Charlestown, T869-469 5473.

Contents

Footnotes

Index

Join us online...

Follow **@FootprintBooks** on Twitter, like **Footprint Books** on **Facebook** and talk travel with us! Ask us questions, speak to our authors, swap stories and be kept up-to-date with travel news, exclusive discounts and fantastic competitions.

Upload your travel pics to our **Flickr** site and inspire others on where to go next.

And don't forget to visit us at